What Happened to MY World?

HELPING CHILDREN COPE WITH NATURAL DISASTER AND CATASTROPHE

By Jim Greenman

Senior Vice President

Bright Horizons Family Solutions

Comfort for Kids, 200 Talcott Ave, Watertown, MA 02472
www.brighthorizons.com

Table of Contents

PART II: HELPING CHILDREN LIVE IN THE WORLD

RESOURCES

Acknowledgments

Many people devoted an enormous amount of time, energy, and heart to make *What Happened to MY World* happen on a greatly accelerated schedule.

For ideas, copy editing, and writing support:
Julie Baker
Nurit Bloom
Susan Brenner
Mary Bresadola
Dixie Bryson
Joy Bunson
Johna DiMuzio
Christine Fossaceca
Laura Guimond
Barbara Levinson
William Pfohl
Griff Samples
Erin Thomas
Kristin Thomas
Craig Thomas
Linda Whitehead
Judy Uhron

For providing the wonderful artwork and selected quotations:
Janine Schueppert, Ashley Bryan, and the kids of the Katrina's Kids Project
www.katrinaskidsproject.org.

For managing the printing process: Andrew Jozwicki and Todd Bone at Wetmore Printing/RRD

Kristen Donahue and Randa Evans deserve special mention for skillfully providing ideas and support, copy editing, and managing the editorial and publishing process.

Debra Cole, Cole Design, Inc. dropped her busy schedule and generously contributed the layout and graphic design.

Anything that is human is mentionable,
and anything that is mentionable
can be more manageable.
When we can talk about our feelings,
they can become less overwhelming,
less upsetting, and less scary.
The people that we trust
with that important talk can help
us know that we are not alone.

FRED ROGERS
(Life's Journeys According to Mister Rogers: Things to Remember Along the Way)

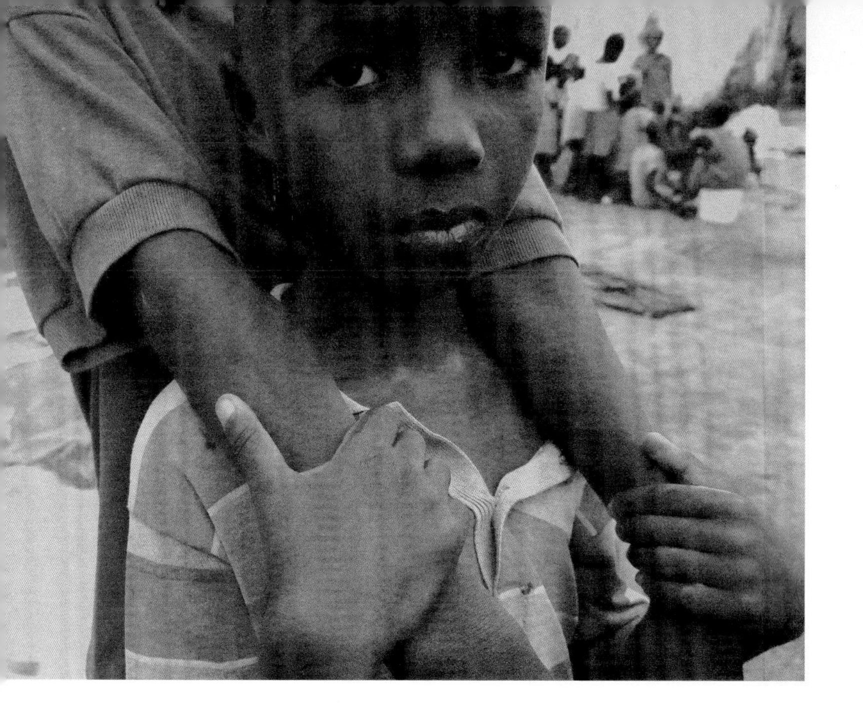

Introduction

Children's lives have always been marked by change. Each day brings new revelations that life is filled with storms as well as sunshine. No child ultimately escapes from the experience of fear, loss, grief, and trauma. But extraordinary events that shatter the sense of security of everyone they know and love put a particular pressure on the adults in their lives to be at their best as parents and caregivers.

In the Fall of 2005, Hurricane Katrina, followed by Hurricane Rita, shattered much more than emotional security by wreaking death and destruction throughout the Gulf Coast region. Together, the hurricanes literally blew away the finely woven fabric of people's lives: their homes, their families, their jobs, their pets, and all the possessions that connect them to the past. Hurricanes Katrina and Rita, like the Asian Tsunami a year earlier, left hundreds of thousands of people uprooted and homeless, adrift in a devastated world.

What Happened to MY World? Helping Children Cope with Natural Disaster and Catastrophe is for parents, teachers, and everyone working to help children and families make sense of a world where the forces of nature and man can unleash a fury in which buildings are torn apart, lives are lost, and our sense of safety and security can disappear in a flash. It is designed to help adults peer into the minds of children, from infancy through the teenage years, and understand their fears, their grief, and their struggles to understand why — whether through acts of nature or human beings — the ground under their feet can disappear and the world can become a very frightening place. It is to help both those who experience and survive catastrophe first hand, as well as the children who witness from a distance and wonder what it was like or whether they will find themselves in similar circumstances.

Extraordinary events like Katrina test us all as citizens and human beings sharing a planet. They test us as parents, both as guardians of our children trying to keep them emotionally safe, and as our children's teachers trying to raise them to become enlightened and empathetic adults. Children learn from what we say and don't say about the world and their place in it, as well as from our actions. Children grow into the kind of people they will become at least in part by how we guide them through their questions, concerns, and fears, and whether we use the teachable moments thrust upon us to guide and teach the children we care for.

What Happened to MY World? is adapted from *What Happened to the World? Helping Children Cope in Turbulent Times* (Greenman, 2001), which was written in response to the events of September 11, 2001. Hurricanes Katrina and Rita and the Asian Tsunami are used here as reference points for helping children learn to cope with disaster and find strength within themselves. Every day, children everywhere are struggling with life's darker side. The insights into children's thinking and behavior, and what they need from the adult world in the aftermath of these events, apply to other calamities, both personal and social: death of loved ones; exposure to violence; the descent into homelessness; or even the sudden loss of a parent due to divorce or separation. Fear, grief, anxiety, and despair have the same disabling force, no matter the cause. The understanding, compassion, and thoughtfulness required by the adults who care for children are much the same. It is easy to support and respect children and parents when they are at their emotional and behavioral best; it's much harder when circumstances beyond their control may have driven them to their worst.

PART I explores how children respond to natural disaster and other catastrophe. Their reactions and what they need from adults are broken down by age.

PART II looks at how children can begin to understand both the world of nature at its most powerful and some difficult aspects of human society exposed when disaster erupts: death, poverty, and racial tension.

The Resources section includes resources for parents and professionals to explore more deeply all the topics introduced in this book. There are Web sites and books for adults and children on coping with stress, understanding the natural world and coping with disasters, addressing questions about poverty and race, and developing plans for survival and recovery.

PART I

Children and Catastrophe

1. What Happened to MY World?

I came from the weather. The weather was bad.

JARED, AGE 5

Jared, like hundreds of thousands of other children, fled Hurricane Katrina. Children like Jared left homes, pets, and predictable lives when their world was suddenly washed away. And like four-year-old Emily, a September 11 survivor, who looked out at the World Trade Center rubble and asked "What happened to the world?" Jared and everyone else touched by catastrophe were thinking the same things:

Will I be OK?
Will you be OK?
Will everyone I love be OK?
Will the world that I know be OK?

Society-Shaking Events

September 11 touched us all because of the surprise and the unimaginable horror of planes crashing into buildings, people disappearing into smoke, and rubble covering the streets. Anyone who felt removed from the threat of terror — who thought that mass destruction happened only in poor countries or far away on the television or movie screen — was forever shaken and changed. Subsequent bombings in Madrid, London, and other places have had the same effect.

Hurricane Katrina and its destructive sister Rita created a similar shock. Hurricanes and floods happen every year, but the scale of Katrina was very different in size and damage, in lives lost and thrown into chaos, and in the inability at all levels to respond effectively to avoid ongoing catastrophic results. The emotional shock went far beyond the areas in Katrina's path. The vast ruin, the images of desperate people on rooftops or makeshift boats, the reports of hunger, thirst, and violence that went on for days, and the bodies floating by or left unattended on the street — how could this be America? So destructive was Katrina that when Rita struck two weeks later and another million people were evacuated and a hundred thousand homes were lost — a significant disaster in its own right — there was widespread relief that it wasn't worse.

Once apon a time there was a storm name Katring. It flooded all the housed & destroyed everyones belongings. It killed some people. It ruined some people lives, it made some people lives better. Some think it happened for a reason. But some people still acting stupid. Some people even made it worse for others. The Super Dome was destroyed. They treated us very terrible. They made us pass out in the sun. They made us eat nasty food out of a bag. We were in a bad percdicument

Super Dome

Brenda

Life Is Not Fair.

Natural disasters and other large-scale tragedies touch many people, but not equally or in the same way. Hundreds of thousands of children experienced the force and damage of the hurricanes directly. Many more were touched through the lives of people they knew. And since we live in a 24-hour pounding news culture where dramatic images of horror or grief surround us constantly, millions more children watched the television thinking, "That could have been me or my friend or relative or someone I love." Others thought, "Why them and not us?" When Hurricane Rita followed on Katrina's heels and the fear of further natural disasters continued, growing with every report on the impact of global warming and the effects of society's impact on the coastlines and flood planes, many could say, "That could be me or someone I love — next time."

Many children who have experienced other hurricanes, floods, tornados, earthquakes, or fires at some time in their past may have been shaken again by Hurricane Katrina. And there are many others already living with personal trauma or overwhelming stress who are especially vulnerable to witnessing new tragedy from near or afar. There are also children and adults whose natural empathy and high sensitivity to tragedy and trauma leave them particularly exposed to pain in times when fear and heartbreak are ever-present.

What happened to the world? It has become a place where we need to support each other and our children as events unfold. When a child experiences a world-altering event, we are the ones called on to provide comfort and security and to help them make some sense of what has happened.

Everyday Horror

Headline-making events like the Gulf Coast Hurricanes, the Asian Tsunami, and September 11 touched almost all of us. But remember that *every day*, untold numbers of children also look around and ask *what happened to my world?* Four-year-old Jorge fleeing with his family from a burning house; seven-year-old Mala watching the tornado blow away her family's home; two-year-old Eric and his mother leaving behind an abusive, alcoholic father; nine-year-old Tonya, her three brothers and sisters, and her mother and grandmother looking for shelter after another eviction; eleven-year-old Mai mourning the death of her father. Whether from natural or man-made disaster, societal or personal tragedy, worlds are shattered every day. The monsters of drug addiction or violence; the misfortune of fires, job lay-offs, or serious illness; and the tragedies of marital conflict, divorce or death — all of these daily tragedies send thousands of families into a sudden descent of confusion, fear, anger and the unknown. The child whose predictable personal world is collapsing will live with the same fear and uncertainty as the child in a national crisis.

When Jared's world washes away and is replaced by a shelter, or Emily's world is demolished, we all are witness. But when the world shatters for Jorge, Mala, Tonya, or Mai and all the other children and their families, there are rarely dramatic pictures of people emerging from the rubble on television. No politicians make visits and issue comforting statements. No celebrities hold benefits. There may or may not be support for their families as daily life goes on for the others around them. But for the individual, the experience of a shattered world is the same whether it's because of a family tragedy or an international event.

There are, of course, differences when a calamity or crisis is personal rather than communal. The sense of isolation and powerlessness may be greater — *how can the world go on as if nothing happened?* On the other hand, a personal tragedy in a caring community might engender more support because the rest of the community is not in crisis. No individual crisis is exactly the same; each of us is different and the circumstances are unique. But the shock, disbelief, grieving, numbness, anger, mood swings, and inability to go about daily life — the need to talk or the need to be silent — are the same. And our needs for security and hope for the future are the same as well.

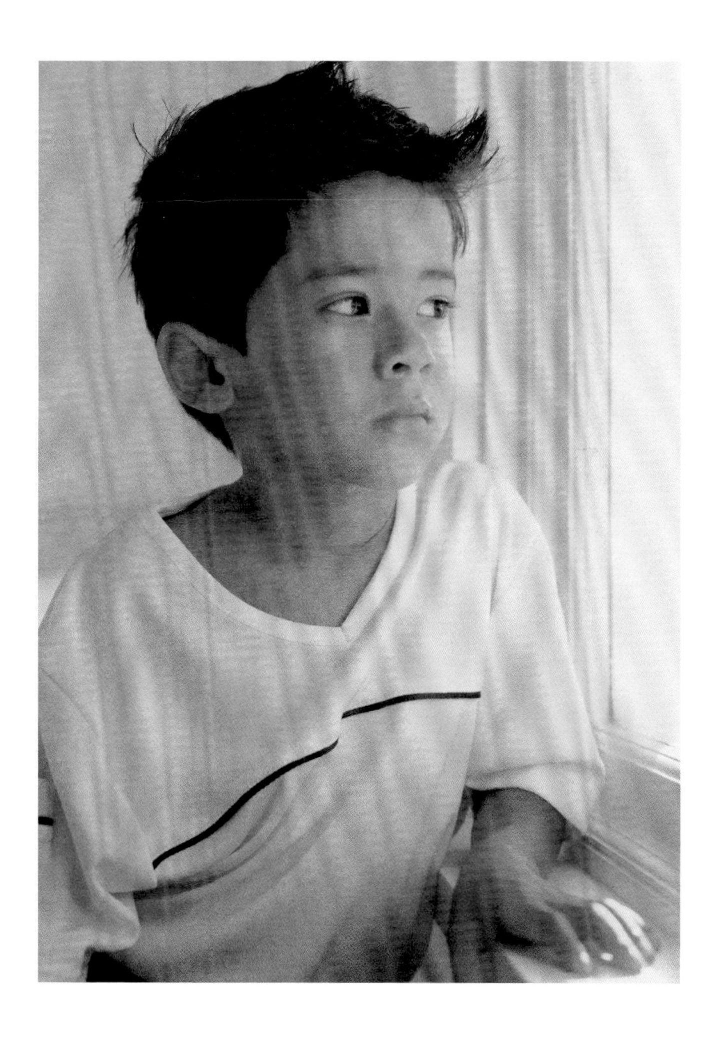

By: Jaleel
New Orlean
Cit

Pillars of Security

There is nothing more basic than the need to feel secure: to feel that I am all right, right here, right now. We feel secure when the world is safe, predictable, and manageable. We know we can fit into that world as ourselves and will be accepted by the people we encounter. We can relax when we are with people we trust, know what to expect, or have confidence that our life experience gives us the skills to cope with whatever will come our way. This is the exact opposite of how we feel in a crisis situation.

Young children are perpetual tourists without much life experience, truly strangers in a strange land. They are developing their minds and bodies at such a rate that they are literally new people with each sunrise. Their backlog of life experience is so slight that each day, each new place, each *old* place brings surprises. Their courage rises and falls like the tides. As we grow up and experience more of the world, good and bad, our life experience gives us more of a base, but we depend on four pillars of security to help us face life's struggles: *people, place, routine, and ritual*:

> *People:* For most of us, the most insecure feeling of all is feeling alone — no hand to hold, no one to look up to, no one to warn us, and no arms to hold us when we stumble. Security comes from familiar and trusted loved ones who know and understand us, and who we know and understand. But if those people are just not themselves and behaving unpredictably (as often happens in crisis), or worse, if we have no one and are surrounded by strangers, a calming sense of security is hard to come by.

Place: In our homes, we can relax. We take comfort in the familiar order, the sounds, sights, and smells. We know our way around and how things work. There are few surprises. Our treasured things are there to reassure us, as are our memories. An unfamiliar place makes demands on our awareness — we need to be alert. In *our* places, we have the freedom to find or create sanctuaries and places to pause.

Routine: Routines are patterns of actions and expectations, the familiar order of the day and the tasks that we do protect us from fear of the unknown. The structuring of time into routines has an enormous impact on how we feel. Routine reassures each of us and stabilizes groups — the regular meal, the prompt dry diaper, the inevitability of sleep.

Ritual: Our individual lives are orderly and meaningful with daily rites that have gained our affection: the first cup of coffee in our favorite cup, goodbye kisses, how we wake up or go to sleep, the routes taken to work or school. Ritual joins routine and the physical order as the bind that holds individuals and groups together in times of stress and uncertainty.

The four pillars are not equal; certainly people matter the most. But place, routine, and ritual are essential and support the first pillar.

When you are a child or an adult in a crisis, all four pillars — people, place, routine, ritual — may become shaky or crumble and your world may feel as though it is crashing down upon you — strange people, strange place, strange routine, and few rituals.

Degrees of Loss and Trauma

My uncle was on the roof but when they came,
when the rescue boats came, they only took
Mommas and kids.

8-YEAR-OLD BOY

Each of the many survivors of Hurricanes Katrina and Rita has a story that deserves to be heard. Many, perhaps most, were brave and terrified at the same time. But the range of trauma is extraordinarily wide. When disaster strikes, many lives are disrupted and lots of people are affected; some firsthand, others from a distance. Lumping survivors together diminishes all the dimensions of the horror that people experienced and continue to face. Some may lose little but their sense of safety and perhaps their optimism; however, neither of these are small losses. Some children drove away from the storm in fear, but with family intact and little lost. People who had a lot to begin with may have lost a great deal, but still have the human or material resources to start over.

At the opposite extreme, some stayed through the storm, terrified, while others were rescued from rooftops. Children were literally plucked out of the floodwaters or floated to safety. Some people (children included) were true heroes, saving others. Some lost loved ones or were separated from their families for weeks afterward (including young children), with no way of knowing their fate. Some people lost key documents or proof of identity: birth certificates, ID's, photographs, financial papers, insurance documents, and school records. Others spent days without food or water, and witnessed death and violence while fearing for their own lives. For many, the sight, the smell, the feel of death will never leave them. And because it has been mentioned by an affluent few that many of the people had little to lose, thus downplaying their misery, just think about what it must be like to lose that "little" everything. While many lost everything and came out of it with spirits intact, depression and despair can come from losing the material substance of your life, however slight.

Children in the Eye of the Storm

Mother Nature is kind of strange. She creates beautiful flowers. I want to draw them. Mother Nature has a real ugly side too.

DONALD, AGE 12, WHOSE MOTHER DROWNED IN HER LIVING ROOM AS HE ESCAPED.

People do not have to have a direct connection to a catastrophe in order to suffer as a result of it. Some children and adults are shaken simply by the surprise, or size, or horror of the event. September 11 left most of us shocked, sickened, angry, and uncertain about the future. Even thousands of miles away, the emotions were real and for some of us, paralyzing. Hurricane Katrina slowly evolved into a nightmare, and the images of so much devastation and so many lives being torn apart shook many children.

Hundreds of thousands of children and families were not only traumatized, but will be living hard lives for months or years to come. Although therapeutic treatments are a part of what they need, even more so these families need to reconstruct their lives: homes, jobs, schools, and stable families.

Low-income people tend to fair even worse in nearly all cases of natural disaster. Without any financial cushion, their shelter is more precarious, their "rainy day" resources non-existent, and their ability to evacuate the scene, as with Katrina, hampered by no place to go and no way to get there. Often their net worth is not in bank accounts or property, but in the personal possessions that they have managed to accumulate: appliances, clothes, furniture, or jewelry.

How many well-off families would have chosen to stay if their escape meant an uncertain bus to an unknown space with hundreds or thousands of others, leaving behind pets and all their assets?

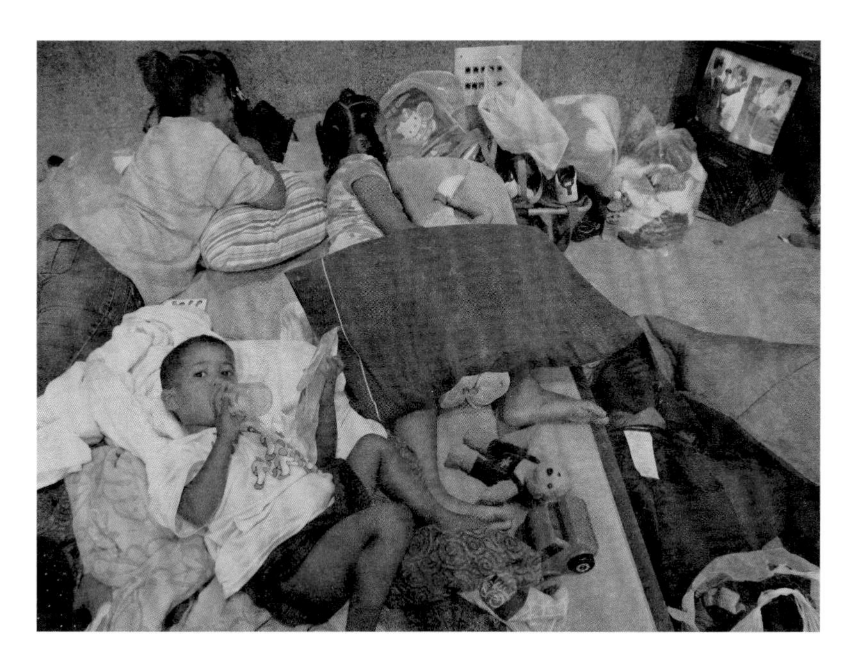

Homelessness

Home is all the words that call you in for dinner,
over to help, into a hug, out of a dream.

MICHAEL J. ROSEN *(HOME: A COLLABORATION OF 30 DISTINGUISHED AUTHORS AND ILLUSTRATORS OF CHILDREN'S BOOKS TO AID THE HOMELESS)*

The ache for home lives in all of us, the safe place
where we can go as we are and not be questioned.

MAYA ANGELOU, *"ALL GOD'S CHILDREN NEED TRAVELING SHOES"*

Imagine what it is like to be a young child without a home, with only the clothes on your back and a sack of stuff that makes up your worldly possessions. If you were a child entering the world of homeless shelters, you would think "What happened to my world?" This scary new world is cramped and clouded by anxiety, uncertainty, and stress. At a shelter, it can be hard to find space to play, things to do, and places to not be in the way. Some days, bright moments can be hard to come by. Some days, it can be sad or scary, boring or chaotic. The adults around you are trying hard to protect you but are often sad or depressed, angry or worried, struggling to cope in an often overwhelming situation. Some days, if you are a kid, it can be hard not to get into trouble, because after all, you are a kid with lots of energy trying to make it through the day.

Imagine if you are that young child's parent, trying to be a good parent and hold on to hope in a difficult situation.

Losing your home is a horrible thing. No matter how meager your home, no matter how few possessions, losing it all of a sudden is an emotional shock. Home is where we can be ourselves, in all our quirky individuality. You can open the refrigerator and get a drink, turn the lights on or off, sift through the photographs and mementos that chronicle your past. You can be silly, or noisy, or crabby. Home is where you have family, pets, plants, closets, toys, and your own blanket and bed.

When children lose their homes in a disaster or personal catastrophe, they may also lose pets and cherished possessions (their collections, trophies, gifts from special people). They might also lose friends, routines, rituals, and even maybe their school. The whole architecture of their lives has collapsed. Children usually have a parent, but a parent in distress, who may be tired from heroic efforts to just make it through the day, or who may be sad or depressed. And when they find shelter, they usually have lost even more: the ability to sleep easily, to keep clean, to get a snack or pocket money, and to move around freely without the constant presence of an adult.

What have children usually found? Crowded conditions, uncertainty and fear, no place to play or do homework, no private space to pause and be off the beaten path. It's hard to keep clean and look good. And older children may have found a social stigma leading to a sense of embarrassment, shame, or anger.

> *The people who ran the shelter left us the MRE's.*
> *An MRE is military food that you*
> *pour water on and it grows.*
>
> 8-YEAR-OLD GIRL

Disaster changes us (and our children) in many ways. We are very glad to be alive and safe. But we are the same people in the aftermath. We are still shy or modest, or very private, or picky eaters, or sensitive to noise or smell, or quirky in all the same ways we are at home. Kids still care about being clean or popular. Kids still want to have the right school supplies and all the things that "normal" kids have. Living in groups of strangers or as guests in the homes of others is difficult.

But helping homeless children begins by looking beyond their loss and current needs and focusing on their strengths. Don't forget what they do have: family, and the human potential for hopes and dreams. They may have families that have survived to this point by small and large acts of courage and determination; families with deep religious faith; or families held together by a strong sense of obligation and love.

Children also have the capacity to survive terrible circumstances. They are living the only life they know. Much more than adults, most children have a resilience and ability to adapt and orient themselves to new circumstances.

It Is Not Always About Trauma

Events like the Gulf Coast Hurricanes, the Asian Tsunami, and other disasters create more than suffering. For some children, the impact is less emotional and traumatic, and more intellectual, political, or spiritual. Why did this happen? How did this happen? What do we do now? To them it might be important or interesting, and they want to know more.

Disasters bring a welcome array of mental health professionals with useful advice on coping with trauma. However, it is important for professionals and parents to not become so focused on trauma that they see it when it isn't even there, and inadvertently induce anxiety when they find reactions that are relatively measured and mild. There will be a variety of reactions, and many of those not significantly affected may feel little more than the desire to continue to live their lives.

2
Children Need Our Strength: How Do We Feel?

Adults largely set the emotional landscape for children. Children depend on us to be strong and solid, to know what is happening, and to guide them through the shoals of troubled waters.

How did you feel undergoing or watching the horror of Hurricane Katrina or the Asian Tsunami? How did you feel after September 11 or the Madrid or London bombings, with the growing realization that the threat of terror had come into all of our lives, that many of us might be directly drawn into the experience of loss? How are you feeling now in a world at war with terrorism, where harm may come through the mail, in our food, in a tall building, in airplanes, or on public transport? Or perhaps in your world, violence or sudden harm has never been a stranger, because of terrorism, crime, warfare, illness, accident, or natural disaster. Once an unexpected tragedy occurs, feelings of vulnerability and insecurity remain for a very long time.

Knowing how *you* feel and finding *your* way to higher ground is critical in order to help the children you love and care for. Even when they are babies, children see, hear, and feel our pain and despair, and they look to us for understanding, reassurance, and hope. They have a sixth sense that detects unease and uncertainty. The first step in helping children cope with catastrophe is to sort through our own feelings and get the support that we need. Children need all the love, strength, and reassurance that we can muster. Their sense of safety stems from us: the big, strong adults who protect them from misfortunes that they never imagined.

The fires destroyed half the houses in the neighborhood, including the one next to ours, and our home was also damaged. It was pretty terrifying. Jasmine was four and she almost immediately seemed to lose a year of development. Always sensitive and cautious, she was now always afraid of everything: lightning, loud noises, cigarettes, us leaving. She wanted to be held, to sleep with us, to keep us home from work. But eight-year-old Ethan began to treat it as a big adventure. He threw himself into clean-up efforts, collected money for the now homeless families, and became a militant on fire safety — reading everything he could and lecturing us on safety. I have to give credit to my wife Susan. She was first relieved, then angry, then relentlessly cheerful, optimistic, and tireless in helping the families who had lost much more than we had. Her patience with Jasmine (and with my worries) kept us going. It took Jasmine nearly a year to become her old self. I guess it took me a little longer. I found myself withdrawing because I got overwhelmed pretty easily with all the paperwork and rebuilding.

A FATHER WHOSE FAMILY ENDURED WILDFIRES IN AUSTRALIA

We all feel and behave differently in response to trauma; the timing and intensity of our feelings and the behavioral changes that follow vary from person to person. Some take it all in a great rush that results in an open wound of emotion; others compartmentalize or push feelings down and try to manage or hide the response. The stress in each of our lives varies widely, as do the supports that we have to offset the large and small challenges to our well-being. But somewhere inside, we all feel frightened and vulnerable. A disaster in which a loved one dies or homes are lost is a different category of trauma altogether. The disaster is not simply a traumatic event; it becomes an ongoing, debilitating, and traumatic existence.

Common Emotional Reactions to Trauma

If you have suddenly lost a loved one, you are in a state of emotional shock and grief. You will have to grieve and then face a new life without the loved one. If you are homeless, you usually arrive at your place of shelter in emotional shock, exhausted, despairing, and disoriented. More important, you don't need to just get over a great loss and restore your spirit; you need to construct a life and home for you and your children.

Shock: How could this happen?

Confusion: What does it all mean?

Fear or worry: What will happen next; where, when, and to whom? Will it end?

Grief: For someone I loved, or someone else like me, or the person I was, or the life I led before.

Anger: At the people behind the tragedy, the people not helping, and at the cruelty and unfairness of it all.

Guilt: Why them and not me? Could I have done more?

Shame and surprise: It's not like me to behave this way: angry, bitter, blaming, or scared.

Helplessness: How can I ever make my world OK again?

Sadness: Lives lost or adrift, children orphaned, futures turned to mud.

Isolation or alienation: I'm probably the only person who feels exactly this way, and I am not sure if anyone understands my feelings.

Hopelessness and despair: I'm not sure my efforts are worth it. What does it matter?

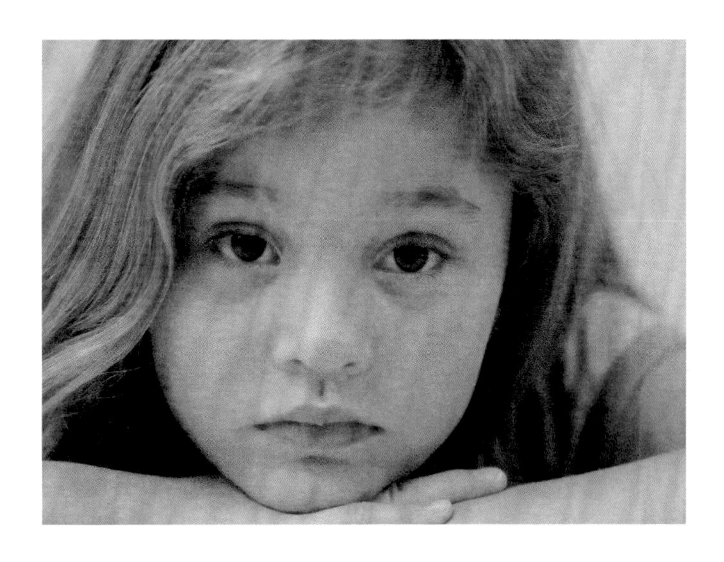

Common Changes in Behavior

I don't know how many times I have been in tears,
or felt really angry.
I feel nothing, like I am far away and I see the kids
and know they want me but have no energy.
I either want to hug my kids or get away from them.
I just want to sleep.
My husband is driving me crazy.
He constantly watches the news,
or just works, and pays little attention to us.
He doesn't sleep much.

Many people respond to trauma with some of the following reactions and changes in behavior:

- Appetite changes
- Change in sleeping patterns
- Anxiety and tension
- Headaches and low resistance to illness
- Crying or depression
- Anger or short temper
- Fatigue or listlessness
- Hyperactivity or mood swings
- Difficulty concentrating
- Numbness or apathy

All of these reactions are normal, up to a point. You are not alone in these responses. But when the reaction is intense and prolonged, seeking help is important for you and the children for whom you care.

Emotional Shock

Direct survivors of catastrophic events often go into the same emotional shock that follows the sudden death of a spouse, parent, or child. They become seriously dazed and confused and exhibit many if not most of the symptoms of trauma for days, weeks, or even longer if the circumstances continue.

To get through this period, survivors need:

- More than a bed. Victims need calm uncluttered surroundings that convey order and safety
- To return to routine instead of generating more change
- Practical, functional help from people, more than help examining their feelings: help with details as small as finding keys to help with insurance and bank accounts
- Help mentally digesting new information — what they need to do, where they need to be
- The stability and reassurance of familiar faces of friends, neighbors, store clerks, and librarians
- To avoid replays of their disaster, or any other disturbing events, as they can reawaken impressions of the all-too-recent catastrophe and rekindle their emotional distress

(Adapted from *Emotional Recovery After Natural Disasters: How to Get Back to a Normal Life* by Ilana Singer)

Note: The plight of families forced into shelter living is magnified because most of what they actually will experience bears little resemblance to the advice above. They may have just a bed, no familiar faces, strange routines, and little support.

Taking Care of Yourself

To take care of children, you need to take care of yourself to the extent that you are able. Some ways to do this are to:

- Accept help from others offering assistance and support with daily responsibilities.
- When ready, talk about your feelings with adults with whom you feel safe; who will really listen without judgment or continual advice.
- Try to create a daily routine and rituals that support your current needs and those of your family.
- Eat right, get exercise and adequate sleep.
- Cry when you need to, and seek solitude when you have to.
- Take breaks from the news and headlines.
- Take breaks from others who bring you down.
- Be gentle with yourself and others and be tolerant of the less-than-ideal behavior of yourself, your children, and others under stress.
- Try to focus on the good things in your days and in your life, and find the seeds of hope.
- Replenish your spirit with friends, faith, family, music, or nature.
- Seek help if you feel that life is not becoming more manageable with time.

After a disaster and especially if one is left homeless, many of the above suggestions are very hard to do. Often the most you can do is try your best to be as gentle and accepting of yourself and others as you are able to be.

3.
Understanding and Supporting Children

"When will the water ever stop?"

5 YEAR-OLD ERNESTO

If you are a child watching the news, it never stops. The waves keep pouring in, flood waters keep rising, planes keep crashing into buildings, buildings keep falling down, bodies keep floating past...day after day. If you happen to be three or four or five years old, still learning to navigate the confusing borders of time and space and what is real and what isn't, you are probably thinking that nature's devastation results in daily destruction. Some children may also be wondering "When will it happen to me?" This is the way many young children think when they see things around them. When a friend's sister dies of cancer, the television news reports a child in a fatal car accident, a cousin no longer lives with her dad, or the news relentlessly sensationalizes a child abduction, a child wonders *"When will it happen to me?"*

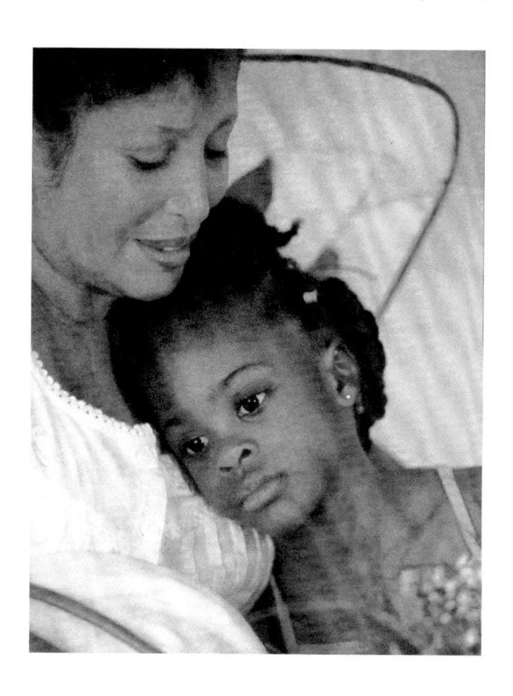

Every Child Is Different

Mara, even at the age of three, paid close attention to TV reports of any threat — crime, hurricanes, and earthquakes — and nightmares always followed. The loss of a pet, a friend moving away, and the sorrows of distant others were all felt intensely and worried over. Alejandro, on the other hand, breezed through his childhood with only a brief pause for the real calamities that occurred around him in his impoverished neighborhood — never imagining it might happen to him. Kyle's vivid imagination and his empathy for others left him seriously vulnerable when any tragedy crossed his path. Troy and Tyrel's nine-year-old responses to airplane crashes or devastating natural disasters were similar. While not appearing particularly upset, each needed precise answers on an infinite number of details about the destruction. And fifteen-year-olds Stephen and Carrie never let on that anything would shake their cool veneer.

Children are different, both from adults and from each other. But taking that seriously *in practice* is not always easy for parents and others who work with children. Children think very differently from adults, and at each stage of development they view the world through their own unique lenses. From birth, children have their own sensitivity to change, to unexpected events, and to distress. They respond to dramatic events and stress in their own way and with differing intensity.

All children are vulnerable, but not equally. A child already grieving over a lost loved one (a person or a pet), divorce, or separation, may be more vulnerable, as will children who have families in crisis, or who are under stress for any number of reasons. Sensitive and empathetic children will also struggle more to come to terms with events that are disturbing.

All children, even babies, will feel the direct effects of natural disaster or family crisis — the emotional upset in the air and the change in people, place, routine, and ritual. Life, as they have come to know it, is disrupted and they are thrown off-center. Supporting children during times of uncertainty and stress begins with knowing the child. The best indicators of distress in children are changes in their behavior. Watch for behavior that is not typical for the child: for example, a normally outgoing child behaving shyly or withdrawing, or a child suddenly becoming clingy, irritable, or anger-prone. A teenager who is normally cool and distant may withdraw from the family even more. A child may regress to past behavior, such as thumb sucking or defiance, being very dependent, or not showing the self-help skills of which he or she is capable.

Remember, *not all behaviors or behavioral changes stem from a crisis.* All the other aspects of life and development are marching on — adjusting to a new grade or school, friends moving away or changing, parents worried about losing their job, or a teenager not having a date — all create personal stress that may eclipse societal turmoil.

Fostering Resiliency

Some children seem to bounce back from terrible circumstances and lead emotionally healthy and productive lives. While a lot may depend on inherited personal qualities: intelligence, an even-tempered nature and independence, among others; resiliency can be nurtured. The key ingredient is at least one caring adult who believes in the child and provides role modeling and support, helping the child see his or her life as positive and valuable. It may be a parent, relative, teacher, family friend, or even an older sibling.

What frightens children in crisis is the feeling of total helplessness, the feeling that they lack any impact on the environment. Those around you may seem defeated. The caring adult who fosters resiliency nurtures in the child a positive outlook and a sense of personal power, and helps the child gain mastery over his or her environment.

In their book *Raising Resilient Children*, Robert Brooks and Sam Goldstein identified the qualities found in resilient children. These children:

- Feel special and appreciated
- Set realistic goals and expectations for themselves
- Solve problems and meet challenges
- Have productive coping strategies that foster growth
- Have a sense of their own strengths and weaknesses
- Feel strong and competent
- Have good interpersonal skills with adults and children
- Focus on aspects of life they can control or influence

They also identified the qualities of caregivers who foster resiliency. They:

- Are empathetic
- Listen and communicate
- Accept children for who they are and help set realistic goals
- Help children feel special and appreciated
- Help children experience positive results and feel competent
- Help children recognize and learn from mistakes
- Develop responsibility, compassion, and a social conscience by providing opportunities to contribute
- Teach how to solve problems and make decisions
- Use discipline and guidance that promotes self-discipline and self-worth
- Change "negative scripts" (thought and behavioral patterns)

If our goal in a crisis is to plant or foster the seeds of resiliency, it is critical to find and support the adults who can play the role of mentor, cheerleader, and guide to the child.

4.
Children Under Three Years Old

They know something is up.

Children under the age of three experience tragedy or disaster that does not directly affect them by absorbing the tension, fear, withdrawal, or pain of the people they love and the changes around them (more motion or stillness, sound or silence, the absence of laughter, even the smell of fear).

Even very young babies react when parents are upset or depressed. Two-year-olds are beginning to understand the concept of pain and may point out hurt people. They also may want to comfort you and others who are upset.

Of course, infants and toddlers will react even more strongly if the tragedy or disaster means the loss of one or more special people, or if it means a huge upheaval in daily routines or a change of environment.

Infants and toddlers can only show their distress with the language of their behavior: being irritable and contrary or clingy and tearful. They often show distress through their daily routines: eating, sleeping, and toileting. Some young children may become listless and apathetic.

What Do Children Under Age Three Need?

- The comfort of the familiar: normal routines and favorite rituals
- A peaceful household (and a peaceful child care experience)
- Very limited exposure to the media and adult conversations about crisis and disaster
- Ample time with calm, loving, reassuring adults

5.
Three to Five Year Olds

They know more than you think, although much of it is incomplete or misconceived.

Like children under three, three to five year olds will react strongly to the loss of loved ones. They too will respond to change of place and upheaval in their daily routines. Three to five year olds are much more aware of events around them than babies and far more aware than we may think they are. However, their understanding is limited. Very young children are magical thinkers and do not live in our adult world. They confuse fantasy and reality, time and space, and are working through the concepts of cause and effect and permanence. The idea of "forever" and death itself are not concepts they understand. Their daily world is already populated with monsters, disasters, nightmares, and heroes. To them, the images on the news are not different from the fictional images they see on the television screen. So the impact of a disaster and its aftermath has the same effect that it has on older children and adults: new fears (of floods, fires, destroyed homes), and anxiety (about strong winds, storms, explosions, earthquakes, or buildings falling down). Young children pay attention to adult feelings and words, and anger or despairing words may make them feel insecure.

Preschool-aged children have a conscious awareness that people can come and go, and in times of crisis they are likely to have fears of abandonment. They feel helpless because they now understand that they do need protection and care, and they worry, "Something might happen to those I love and need."

Children's sensitivity to close calls or tragic events as depicted on television varies widely. While some children barely notice or shake

it off relatively quickly, others are very traumatized. Most children fall in between those extremes. They may ask a lot of questions for which they need honest answers. But they don't need disturbing details or a discussion of issues that don't appear to be on their mind. Do listen for hidden questions. Remember the old story about the five year old who asked, "Where did I come from?" After listening to an explicit description of where babies come from, the child said, "OK, but Tony came from Canada. What about me?"
Play is the way that children make sense of and come to terms with a world that offers surprises and puzzles every day. Play is the way children achieve mastery over the situations in which they are powerless. After tsunamis, floods, fires, or tornados, or when their lives are touched by violence or death, expect children to work out their thoughts and feelings in play representing the power of nature and the heroes in helicopters and boats.

The children were playing Hurricane Katrina. They had all of the farm animals out and were moving them to the second floor as the flood waters were rising. Then they put the baby cow on top of the roof to be rescued but the mama cow was crying because she did not know where her baby was going.

When given the chance children will also use art to work through and express thoughts and feelings. More than a few parents learn of their seemingly oblivious young child's knowledge of calamity, war, or terrorism through their child's pictures of destruction or victims. Preschool children need adults who recognize that playing through (working through) life's horrors is normal, who listen to them, and who do not react harshly, preach, or condemn. Children need to play at being powerful, even evil. Unless play might lead to a child getting hurt physically or emotionally, it is usually best not to intervene, even when their play offends our sensibilities.

Common Preschool Reactions to Stress

- Bedwetting
- Fear of the dark, monsters, or animals
- Clinging to familiar adults
- Nightmares
- Toileting accidents — loss of bladder or bowel control, constipation
- Speech difficulties (for example, being at a loss for words or stammering)
- Loss or increase of appetite
- Cries or screams for help
- Fear of being left alone; fear of strangers
- Confusion
- Behavior that tests others

It is normal for these behaviors to occur from time to time in preschool age children. The key to determining if they represent trauma is to look for changes in a particular child's behavior and for new patterns.

What Do Children Under Age Five Need?

- Normal routines and favorite rituals
- A peaceful household (and a peaceful child care experience)
- Limited exposure to both the media and adult conversations about the crisis
- Ample time with calm, loving, reassuring adults
- Much verbal reassurance that you and they will be OK (but acknowledging they may be scared and are not feeling OK now)
- Plenty of physical reassurance (for example, hugs and cuddles)
- Knowledge of where you and the others whom they love are at any given time
- Opportunities for you to listen, have gentle conversation, and share your own feelings
- Opportunities to play and draw or use other media to express themselves
- Opportunities for and acceptance of play that may reflect the current events with intervention only to avoid harm
- Special time and reassurance at bedtime, including letting the child sleep with you
- Opportunities to be away from the situation and respite from the focus on the crisis or tragedy
- Opportunities to be physically active

- Opportunities to help others and improve the environment
- Help seeing ahead and preparing for the future

6. Primary School-Age Children

They know much more than you think and want to know more.

As children go the through the school-age years, they increasingly inhabit the world outside the home. They can understand what is real and what is permanent, but they lack perspective. They are learning how events fit together and want to understand how things happen and what impact events will have. They have a lot of questions and expect honest answers about details that matter to them. They understand loss and can identify with the people directly affected by events. They can think about what life is like for others. Their fears are real and realistic from their limited perspective, and they often focus on the fact that bad things could happen to them.

It is a time when they are imagining their adult selves — what they will do when they grow up — and identifying with adult roles. In times of crisis, dramatic and powerful heroes and villains both hold fascination for them. They may find great interest in the rescues they experience or see on screen with boats or helicopters. Increasingly, peers play a larger role in shaping thinking, feelings, and reactions to events.

School-age children are interested in rules and the difference between good and bad, right and wrong. Their sense of fairness and justice can lead to outrage and strong, rigid opinions in the face of injustice and terrible acts. When crisis hits their family or community, they often want to help.

When we was walking through all the water and it was getting higher and I was holding on to Tyrell, I wanted to be Superman fly up and then go real fast and get all the people away from the water.

10-YEAR-OLD BOY

Common School-Age Reactions to Stress

- Nail biting or thumb sucking
- Irritability, whining, clinging
- Aggressive behavior at home or school
- Competition with younger siblings for parental attention
- Night terrors, nightmares, fear of the dark
- Avoiding school
- Loss of interest and poor concentration in school
- Withdrawal from peers
- Regressive behavior (reverting to past behaviors)
- Headaches or other physical complaints
- Depression
- Fears about recurring or new disasters
- A need to take on more responsibility for the family and care for others

What Do School-Age Children Need?

- Normal routines and favorite rituals
- A peaceful household (and school experience)
- Ample opportunities for time with calm, loving, reassuring adults
- Adults who will find out what is on their minds, listen, answer their questions honestly with the details that matter to them, and adults who share their own feelings
- Verbal and physical reassurance that you and they will be OK (and acceptance that you and they may be scared and not OK now)
- Knowledge of where the people they love are at any given time
- Guided exposure to the news media and adult discussion
- Opportunities to talk and play with peers and adults
- Opportunities to use art materials or take part in drama to express themselves
- Opportunities to be physically active
- Acceptance from adults of play and dramatic conversation that reflect the current events in their lives and the feelings associated with them
- Relaxed expectations at school or at home during the crisis period

- Reassurance at bedtime, including letting the child sleep with you
- Recognition of their efforts during the disaster
- Opportunities to help others and participate in community efforts
- Help predicting and preparing safety measures to be taken in future disasters
- Opportunities to be away from the situation and respite from the focus on the crisis or tragedy.

7. Teenagers

They know much more than you think and want to know more, but not always from you, and they may or may not want to share their thoughts and feelings — with you.

As children develop through their teenage years, their ways of being in the world and responding to traumatic events change slowly from the reactions of a child to the reactions of a young adult. Teenagers often feel overwhelmed by their emotions, even in normal times. They can experience a vast spectrum of ups and downs. Disasters or violent acts add to the mix because they want to be powerful but often feel the opposite. Peers are critically important, and the group reaction can heighten anxieties or leave a child feeling alone and out of step. Teenagers may respond to traumatic events with either extreme, intense reactions or professed indifference, particularly toward adults. Some will be glued to the television and pore over newspapers and magazines; others will avoid the news. Some may have difficulty expressing caring, concern, and anxiety, while inside they may feel inadequate or guilty. Teenagers often will monitor adult views closely, particularly around bravery, justice, and prejudice. Older teenagers may worry about what the future holds for them in a world where nature's wrath is likely.

Disasters are difficult for teenagers because they occur at the time of life when they are often beginning to move away from family. They are trying to develop a life in school and teen society. If the world of school is disrupted, or the needs of adults to draw family together grows and peer contact diminishes, teens may struggle.

The direct experience of a disaster may provide teenagers with the opportunity to take responsibility for family and others, and to test out their growing maturity. In doing so, their emotional strength may have increased. But if things didn't go as they expected, despite their efforts, it might have left them with feelings of guilt or inadequacy.

Common Teenage Reactions to Stress

- Appetite and sleep disturbances
- Headaches or other physical complaints
- Increase or decrease in energy level
- Indifference, withdrawal, or isolation
- A reduced sense of a future, loss of optimism
- Dark humor, cynicism, or depression
- Confusion/poor concentration
- Poor performance at school or truancy, fighting, withdrawal, loss of interest, attention-seeking behaviors
- Risk-taking behavior or a fear of taking risks
- Rebellion in the home, aggressive behavior
- Refusal to be cooperative

If you have ever been sad, really sad, you know what I am talking about. Sadness is with you all the time. Even when your friends are trying to make you laugh. Sadness seems to be waiting right behind your smile.

BARBARA PARKS, *THE KID IN THE RED JACKET*

What Do Teenagers Need?

- A peaceful household (or school experience)
- To know that you are there for them when they need it (and want it) on their terms. This may mean, for example, late at night or after a period of "hanging out" together
- To know your whereabouts (even if they don't admit it)
- Your willingness to engage in serious discussions
- To be offered opportunities to talk about feelings — yours and theirs — honestly, but without adults being intrusive and with adults listening rather than lecturing
- Opportunities for them to talk about their feelings about natural disaster, the environment, poverty, religion, justice, tolerance, and other social, political, or religious issues.
- Your best and wisest adult perspective on serious issue and your acceptance of their views
- Time with peers for play and discussion
- Opportunities to be physically active
- Adults who encourage participation in social activities, athletics, clubs, etc.

- Opportunities to help others and be involved in the response to crisis
- Group planning for safety measures to be taken in future disasters
- Structured but undemanding responsibilities
- Encouragement and support to take care of themselves: eating well, sleeping sufficiently, exercising regularly
- Temporarily relaxed expectations of performance
- Individual attention and consideration when they ask for it
- Opportunities to be away from the situation and respite from the focus on the crisis or tragedy
- Recognition of their growing competence, maturity, and any of their efforts during the disaster
- Opportunities to take responsibility, help others, or improve the environment
- Help predicting and preparing safety measures to be taken in future disasters

8.
Ways To Help Children Cope With Stress: A Quick Summary*

1. Be available.
2. Listen, listen, and listen some more.
3. Be honest and answer their questions — at their level.
4. Respect differences in children — individual and age based.
5. Encourage consistency, everyday routines, and favorite rituals.
6. Make the environment safe for talking about feelings and thoughts.
7. Expect and allow for all kinds of emotion.
8. Give choices and be flexible — avoid power struggles.
9. Allow a lot of opportunities and different media for expression.
10. Encourage activity and play.
11. Support the child's friendships and social network.
12. Be a model as a human being.
13. Hug with permission.
14. Practice patience.

15. Support children — even when they're at their worst.

16. Expect behavior that is typical of a younger child.

17. Expect behavior that is beyond the child's years.

18. Help them to live right — eat, rest, sleep.

19. Make bedtime special.

20. Resist overprotection.

21. Don't force conversation and interaction.

22. Understand that playing is a way to grieve and sort through fears and confusion.

23. Attend to their physical symptoms of stress.

24. Reassure the child that he or she is not alone.

25. Set limits on acceptable behavior, and enforce them.

26. Remember triggers that will cause distress.

27. Plan family time together.

28. Be available for help if needed.

29. Take care of yourself.

* This list was adapted from *35 Ways to Help a Grieving Child* (The Dougy Center for Grieving Children).

There is no magic formula or single right way to respond to a child in crisis. It is important to know and respect each child's way of coping, even when it is different from our own.

9.
When to Seek Help

Reactions to traumatic events may appear immediately or after several days or weeks. Most of the time, the symptoms detailed above will begin to disappear as the child and family readjust. But for children who experience disaster directly and intensely, or if symptoms accumulate or persist over time, it is wise to seek help outside the family with a counseling service, a religious advisor, a community health center, or through the children's school. A counselor will talk to your children to help them understand their feelings.

Helping Children Live in the World

What kind of people do we want our children to become?

Children need our views about life, the natural world, and social issues articulated in language they are developmentally able to understand. They observe not just what we say but what we do. How and what we teach our children depends on who we are: our civic nature, our spirituality, and our willingness to learn about events, respond with compassion and generosity, and pass that empathy on to our children.

1. Helping Children Understand Natural Disaster and Catastrophe

When crisis or catastrophe envelops our children's world, the most important thing we can do, after ensuring their physical safety, is to be thoughtful and responsive to their emotional and educational needs. The family is a safe haven where children can express their ideas and fears with assurance that their parents will protect them and teach them about the world that they will inherit.

Children's Understanding of the Natural World

Our planet is a wonderful place for life. The natural world: the earth, sun, wind, water, and fire all work together to make it possible for us to live. But nature is far more powerful than human beings, and there are times that natural events create terrible conditions for people. Understanding and respecting the planet and all its forces of nature is important to safe living.

All but the very youngest children can learn that nature is a powerful force in shaping and sustaining life on the planet. Children need to understand that all the powers and properties of nature are interrelated. Human beings are just one part of it. There is a purpose for natural phenomena, and even the most negative events can have positive effects: floods distribute soil to farmland, for example, and fires help create new forest growth. Here are some ways to help children learn to respect the natural world and feel our relationship to the earth:

- Expose children to the outdoor world of streams, rivers, lakes, the ocean, stormy weather, hills, and mountains so that they develop a sense of familiarity and safety in the presence of natural forces.

- Involve children in gardening to help them understand natural cycles.

- Use books, the media, and the internet to explore the world of nature and environmental issues as well as learn about catastrophic events. Learn how floods, forest fires, earthquakes, hurricanes, and other natural phenomenon have a purpose in maintaining the health of the planet.

- As a family, become more aware and active around environmental issues and become activists in promoting policies that respect nature and reduce the likelihood of damage to the environment and destruction to human society.

Children's Fears

It has an eye you know, not a mouth — an evil eye.

DAYSHA, AGE 7, DRAWING THE EYE OF A HURRICANE

Many of the questions and concerns that surface in times of crisis have at their heart the fundamental questions. *Will I be OK? Will you be OK? Will everyone I know and love be OK? Will the world that I know be OK?* Help the child:

- Identify his or her own fears through gentle conversation that follows the child's lead.
- Always try to be realistic while reassuring the child that it is unlikely the catastrophe will happen again the same way. Assure the child that if there is a next time, "We will be ready" (even if you are not feeling entirely sure yourself).
- Respect the child's fears and remember that fear is not always rational.

In the aftermath of natural disasters, many children and adults will increase their fear of storms, floods, tornados, and earthquakes. With young children, the best way to break down the fear is through your strong, calm, thoughtful presence. Older children also rely upon the strong presence of adults and their rationality and optimism. Children need to hear that:

- People are working very hard to learn more about early warnings of natural disasters and ways to prevent loss of life and damage to society.
- Our family knows what to do if we are in any danger.
- As a family, we will devise plans to always be prepared and safe.

2.
Answering Children's Questions

The aftermath of any disaster leaves us with hard questions to answer. Children need the opportunity to talk about the emotions and issues that are in the air around them. As they get older and their understanding of the world outside their home grows, they also need our honest answers to the larger issues: "Why is life so unpredictable?" "Why do natural and manmade disasters create catastrophe and tragedy?" "Why do innocent people die?" "Are some people more vulnerable than others?" "Can't we do something to help those more unfortunate people?"

Some questions may test our fundamental social, political, and religious views: "Is nature mad at us?" "Why do some people die and some live?" "Why were so many faces of Katrina's victims Black?" "Why can't people be saved faster?" "Why does our family have so much and there are many families that are hungry and have nothing?" "Why did we lose everything we had?"

"How come we couldn't save Granmomma or my dog Sneaky?"

AMANI, AGE 6

Children need our best answers, or our honest lack of an answer. Sometimes all we can say is that "Bad things happen to good people and we don't know why." They need our thoughtfulness and willingness to help them seek answers. *No child will ever thank us for lying to him or avoiding her questions.*

Before Talking to Children

Even if we only have a moment to think about what to say and how to say it, try to remember to:

- Get your own feelings and thoughts straight. Have another adult listen to you first if you aren't sure you are ready to talk to your child.
- Try to be your most thoughtful, calm, and emotionally stable self when you talk to children. Be prepared for the inevitable difficult questions about what bad things could happen to us, why people die, and why some people live.
- Think not only about what you want to say, but also about how you want it to come across.
- Watch your words, tone, and body language. You may give a nonverbal message of calm, sadness, anger, confusion, or indifference.
- Ask children what they think the words that they are using or hearing mean: *death, drowning, loss, weather, disaster, hurricane, looter, hero.*
- Understand what they already know and feel before beginning any dialogue by asking "What are you thinking and feeling?"
- Find natural opportunities to ask what's on the child's mind and follow his or her lead. Recognize the clues in a child's art, play, or conversations with friends. Accept his or her feelings.

- Check first before assuming either a lack of or strong interest. When you encourage a young child to draw, play, or talk about his or her feelings, you give permission to freely express scary or angry thoughts.

- Honestly share your feelings, but always try to be in control of your emotions in the presence of your children.

- Be strong in a crisis even when feeling sad, scared, confused, or angry. The child needs to draw upon your strength, not take care of you.

- Provide the child hope by simply sharing hugs or reassuring smiles that say, "I'm here for you and we will make it through this." While a young child may need to hear, "Lots of strong, smart people are working hard to keep us safe," an older child may need to help you plan what to do or help research efforts to prevent natural disasters.

- Try to monitor children's exposure to media coverage of disasters and crises. Children have not seen much of life or weathered many storms and can easily feel that everything, everyone, everywhere is coming apart. The quantity and intensity of television, radio, and newspaper coverage as well as adult conversation during a crisis can easily frighten children, and adults should try to manage those images. Very young children often do not understand that one incident generates weeks of repeated images. Not only did Hurricane Katrina, the Asian Tsunami, and September 11 generate fearful images, but tornados, hurricanes, forest fires and the sensational treatment of child abductions and murder do so as well. This can magnify the child's sense of the world as a menacing place.

- Respect the growing ability of school-age children and teenagers to understand and discuss issues openly and honestly.

- Consider that natural disasters such as hurricanes and tsunamis will spark an interest in environmental concerns as well as issues of poverty and race for older children.

Stay tuned in to your child.

- Keep listening, asking, conversing with, and reassuring the child as his or her thoughts and feelings evolve. Remember that every child is different. The explanation of national, global, or personal events needs to match the child's developmental understanding and personality. Don't give more information than the child is ready for.

Protect your child's idealism.

- Children are born idealists. For them, the world is a good place where nature is usually friendly and predictable, people are mostly good, and life is worth living. Sudden exposure to catastrophe or violence tests their idealism and optimism as well as ours. If children are exposed to too much of life's dark side, they may lose their sense of optimism.

Stay alert to signs of stereotyping and racism.

- In times of conflict or exposure to societal issues, "us versus them" mentalities, ethnic and social class stereotypes, and contempt for behaviors different from our own may lead to racism and cultural bias. Though often unintentional, this can be damaging nonetheless. More than ever, we need to teach children to accept and respect cultural and social groups different than

theirs and see the good in other people. Children need us to model tolerance, respect for diversity, and an interest in learning about other people, cultures, and countries. In every conversation work toward greater understanding across ethnic, cultural, and social class lines. Be at your best as a human being.

Steer your child toward helping actively.

- The feelings of powerlessness and helplessness shared both by children and adults after a crisis are alleviated through action. Our sense of power is restored by taking steps to improve our own current situation or to increase our preparedness for future situations. Finding ways to connect with others in the community and around the world to show our common humanity has the same result. Some ways to do this include finding pen pals, fundraising or donating money, cultural exchanges, and cross-community clean up or work projects.

3.
Answering Questions about Natural Disasters

That river —it was full of good and evil together. It would water the fields when it was curbed, but then if an inch were allowed it, it crashed through like a roaring dragon.

PEARL S. BUCK (*THE OLD DEMON*)

What is a hurricane?

For preschool children:

Hurricanes are big storms with lots of rain and really strong winds. Sometimes everything gets flooded and lots of things get knocked down. We will need to go to a safe place or get away from the storm. *We can get ready ahead of time to be safe. We will be safe if it happens again!*

For older children:

A hurricane is a powerful tropical storm that comes in from the ocean and brings lots of rain, lightening, and very high whirling winds of 75 to 180 miles an hour (as fast as a race car). They are also called tropical cyclones or typhoons and they get their energy from warm tropical water before they head to land, called *making landfall.* Hurricanes have the power of the most powerful bombs. Hurricanes often cause flooding and tornados. They hit the Caribbean islands, the East and Gulf coasts of the United States, and the Far East, Pacific Islands, India, Japan, and Northern Australia. In the United States, hurricane season is from June to November.

Hurricanes happen every year when the surface waters are warmest; some are much stronger than others. Hurricanes are more destructive in the United States today than 50 years ago. Today there are more people living on coastal areas in low-lying areas where hurricanes do the most damage. And wetlands, which work like a sponge and help reduce a hurricane's power, have been replaced by development. These changes may be increasing the force and impact of hurricanes.

Hurricanes are predictable and can be tracked. Families and communities can prepare for hurricanes to make sure that no one gets hurt and property is protected. *Our family will make sure that we are prepared for the next one.*

What is a flood?

For preschool children:

Floods are when there is so much water that water covers everything.

For older children:

A flood is when lots of water flows into a dry area. Too much rain causes rivers, streams, or lakes to overflow their banks and flood surrounding areas. High ocean levels and high waves can also cause a flood. Sometimes the structures used to control flooding such as dams, levees, or floodwalls break and the water released floods an area. A *flash flood* happens all of a sudden after a sudden rain.

Floods usually take time to develop, and the location can be predicted and planned for. Floods happen because water flows downhill due to gravity. People who live in areas where flooding is common can be careful and plan to escape when floods are likely.

What is a tornado?

For preschool children:

Tornados are very strong storms with winds that that can knock down anything. They are called "twisters" because the wind twists and twirls around. When there are tornado warnings, everyone needs to go to the place that keeps them safe; usually a basement or a room of the house with no windows.

For older children:

Tornados form from thunderclouds and are the most powerful storm for their size. They have very fast swirling, twisting, sucking winds of up to 300 miles an hour (almost as fast as a jet). Unlike hurricanes, which swirl outward, tornados or twisters swirl inward and rotate around a funnel of low pressure. They look like upside-down cones. Tornados usually move along above the surface at 35 to 50 miles per hour (mph) but can go up to 70 mph. When they touch down, they can suck up and destroy everything in their path: trees, trucks, bridges, houses and other buildings, and even farm animals. A tornado's path may be a mile or two or up to hundreds of miles. Most tornados strike in the United States in April, May, and June.

Tornados develop quickly out of a storm, and sometimes there is little warning that a storm has developed twisters. But people can be safe by listening for warning sirens and radios or television announcements, as well as having a safe place identified to quickly go to if tornados are in the area.

What is an earthquake?

For preschool children:

An earthquake is when the ground starts shaking. The shaking may shatter buildings or break up roads. Or the ground may develop big cracks or holes. Many people are working to protect us from earthquakes and to help us be prepared.

For older children:

The Earth is divided into three layers: the core, the mantle, and the crust. Deep in the middle is a solid metal core which is very hot, and also an outer core which is liquid. The outer core is about 1,300 miles thick and the inner core is about 800 miles to the center of the earth. Next is a layer of hot minerals, called the mantle, which is flexible like plastic. The top layer is called the crust. All the oceans and the land are the top of the crust. The crust is typically about 25 miles thick beneath continents, and about 6.5 miles thick beneath oceans. The crust is relatively light and brittle. Most earthquakes occur within the crust.

Under the crust are tectonic plates made out of rock. These plates move all the time, but so slowly we can't even feel it. The breaks in between the plates are called faults. Sometimes, a plate rubs or bumps into another and this causes an earthquake. Earthquakes create shocks and aftershocks that can be large or small. We may not even notice all the small earthquakes, but large earthquakes have destroyed cities and killed thousands of people.

Scientists are working hard to learn more about how to predict earthquakes and warn people. They are also working on how to protect buildings and other structures so that they can reduce the damage to life and property.

What is a tsunami?

For preschool children:

A tsunami is an earthquake that happens beneath the sea. The earthquake can cause a big wave to form that can come onto the land and cause floods.

For older children:

A tsunami or *tidal wave* is a giant wave of water up to hundreds of feet high (as big as a big building) that rolls to the shore and knocks down and floods anything in its path. The bigger the tsunami, the farther the wave will reach on the shore and flood more land. Scientists hope to find ways to give people in coastal areas more warning before a tsunami strikes so that they can move farther away and to higher areas.

What is a mudslide?

Mudslides happen when rain or flooding fills the earth on the sides of hills or mountains with water. The solid ground becomes mud and slides down the hill, taking trees, buildings, and everything else down the slope.

People who live on hills or steep slopes can plan to get out safely as the ground gets full of water, before the mud begins to slide down the hill.

What is a wildfire?

Wildfires are fires that cover a large area where there has been very little rain and all the trees and shrubs are dry. They can happen just as easily in housing developments as in forests. When the winds are strong, the fire can be carried by the wind and then destroy an even bigger area. Wildfires usually happen in late summer and fall in areas where rain is scarce. Terrible wildfires have happened in Los Angeles, parts of Australia, and other dry areas. They can start because of lightning, careless people who drop cigarettes or forget to put out campfires, or other reasons. They can last for days or even months.

We can know when fires are likely to happen, and families can work to protect their houses and prepare to flee to safety.

4.
Answering the Questions of Child Survivors

I was really scared during that Katrina storm. I could have been braver 'cause I didn't go find my dog Jo Jo who I hope we find if we go back to Orleans. But I was brave when helping my Auntie with baby Jalen on the bus when that other hurricane made us leave. I hate the wind.

JAZMYNE, AGE 9

Everyone was scared, even the wonderful people who rescued others. Some were probably both scared and brave at the same time. Lots of people stayed scared for a long time and still have nightmares and scary thoughts. Police officers, firefighters, and the soldiers all feel scared sometimes too.

We Survived
Katrina !!
Man look at my car
Man this Downbad

How can I feel better if I had to leave my home?

FEMA for Kids (http://www.fema.gov/kids/feel.htm) suggests that kids try to remember six things:

1. Disasters don't last very long. Soon, things will be back to normal.

2. You can get a new routine if you can't go home for awhile. You will settle down into a new place and you will meet new friends.

3. Look to your parents or other adults for help when you feel scared or confused. They will help you understand what is happening. Don't be afraid to ask questions.

4. Sometimes it helps to write about your experiences or to draw pictures about what has happened. You can describe what happened and how you feel. The FEMA for Kids Web site can post your projects.

5. It's OK to cry during a disaster, but remember, it will get better.

6. You may be able to help out. Children of all ages can help in the shelter by babysitting other children or cleaning up or serving food. You can even help with sandbagging or cleaning up your house after a tornado or hurricane or earthquake.

My mom is really sad and not herself. Sometimes I think it is my fault. What can I do?

Even if you are not the perfect kid in the time of crisis, how your Mom feels is not your fault! When it's a bad time for your Mom, try to be helpful and not get in her way. She has a lot on her mind and, like you, is feeling sad and trying to figure out what to do. She will get better and will keep you safe.

I miss my ______ (relative, friend, pet). What can I do?

Remember all the good things about____. Draw some pictures, tell some stories and let yourself cry. If your ____ is separated from you or missing, don't give up hope that everything will work out. Remember that _____ loved you, and you will always have special memories of your time together. It's OK to still talk to ____ or act out what you would say if ____ were still here.

5. Answering Children's Questions about Death

Nobody ever told me that grief felt so much like fear.

C.S. LEWIS (A GRIEF OBSERVED)

For every age, the answer is a developmentally appropriate version of "Everything that is alive dies sometimes. Death is a part of life." Natural disasters, as with terrorism or war, bring the idea and reality of death to the foreground of children's lives. Adults create a climate of security or insecurity by their behaviors. If children experience a wall of silence or a storm of grief, they may not feel able to ask questions. Adults need to try to establish an atmosphere where children's feelings, questions, and needs are taken into account.

Why do people (or pets) die?

While it is very sad when people or animals that we care about die, we need to remember how wonderful it was to have our time with them and keep them alive in our memories. Children under three years old experience the death of a loved one as an unsettling absence or the presence of sadness or emotional turmoil around them. They simply need our presence, warmth, and strength. Older children need the same, but also our understanding of their feelings.

To preschool children, death is another mysterious part of life. If someone who cares for them dies, they often feel abandoned. *It is the absence that counts* because they don't understand the finality of death or the emotional weight of grieving. The death of others is mostly a big deal to them because it is important to us; it upsets them because it upsets us. In a classic *Sesame Street* episode, Big Bird had to face the death of Mr. Hooper following the relatively sudden death of the actor playing the beloved character. He was told gently by Gordon that Mr. Hooper died and will have to live on in our memories. Big Bird asked some questions and was very sad. The next day, however, Big Bird saw Gordon and asked him where he could find Mr. Hooper. Gordon gently reminded him that Mr. Hooper had passed away and would not be back. In a horrified voice, Big Bird said, "Never?" and burst into tears.

Because young children believe the world revolves around them, they may feel that a death was something that they caused. They need reassurance that the person's absence is not the result of their own actions or feelings.

Older children understand that death is permanent and share our struggle with coming to terms with the "why" of it," "why now," and "how will we carry on and get over it." Their grief and sadness can be as deep as our own if it is someone they love. They can begin to identify with the loss that others experience. The knowledge that death is final leaves them wondering about their own death and the possible deaths of people they know. They may feel that death is a punishment for those who died or their loved ones. Reading books and having conversations both prior to and after the death of a loved one can help children understand that death is part of the cycle of life. Death is also simply interesting to school age children. They are often fascinated with the cause and the details of the death and its aftermath. They understand death as a physical experience and often are concerned about the body, as many preschool aged children would be as well: What happened to it? What will happen to it now?

Children and families who have or are experiencing the death of a loved one under traumatic circumstances need to draw on extended family and friends for support. They should also take advantage of the resources provided by employers and community agencies and the materials listed in the resources section at the end of this guide.

6.
Answering Children's Questions about Poverty

Hurricane Katrina brought out into the open the sad reality that there are many poor people in America. Many children (and adults all over the world) were shocked by this. How could there be so many poor people in such a rich nation? Poor people are often invisible to middle-class America and the world. They live in different neighborhoods and are rarely on television unless portrayed as problems or threats.

Poverty is an important problem. The United States poverty rate of around 12% is the highest in the developed world. There are more than 37 million people below the poverty line, equal to the entire population of Canada.

Because of what they see on television, children may associate poverty with race. Children should know that poor people in the United States (and the world) come in all colors and ages, but children and old people make up the highest percentage. There are more poor whites than African Americans or Hispanics. However, a much higher percentage of African Americans and Hispanics are poor.

Why are people poor?

There are children and families all over the world who don't have enough to eat or a place to live. Most poor people are hard working but have very low wages and they don't come from families with money in the bank. Some people live in areas where there are few jobs and the land or climate makes farming difficult. In some places in the world, and even in parts of America, almost everyone is poor. For most poor people and all poor children, it is not their fault that they are poor.

As a matter of fact, in some cases people who are or have been poor have many strengths that those who are better off may not have, such as resourcefulness in surviving terrible conditions, generosity and deep caring, and connections with others. For example, low-income people tend to give a much higher percentage of their income to charity than the affluent do.

How you answer older children further will depend on your political views and religion. We all agree that family counts a lot, in one way or another. Children are born into their circumstances. Sometimes luck is an important factor. Sometimes people make bad choices. You might believe that poor people need more economic support and opportunity. You may believe that culture has more to do with it than economics and we need to help to change poor people's way of thinking and behaving. Most believe that economics and culture are interconnected. If you are religious, you might also believe that God plays an important role in the fate of people and that the individual's spirituality is a factor in his or her success or failure.

How can I help people who don't have as much as I have?

There are many ways we can help share what we have with children and families who are less fortunate and whose situation touches our hearts:

- Raise money for people who are in need because of disasters or war.

- Donate what we don't need for the poor people in our town, contribute to food shelves, clothing drives, and holiday giving.

- Get involved with groups like Habitat for Humanity, which builds homes for those without them, or Heifer International, which helps poor communities begin to be able to produce their own food.

- Help to stop the misrepresentation and false stereotyping by not judging poor people or assuming that they are lazy, stupid, or bad.

- Do you have any ideas?

The TV talked a lot about looters and gangs of men with guns. Why did people steal after the storm or flood?

Every community has a very small number of bad people who do bad things even during a horrible catastrophe when people are suffering. But some others who are not bad might get called criminals or looters even though they are just trying to find food, water, and clothing to survive. Often, bias and prejudice is involved in who gets called "looters" and who is portrayed as "doing what they need to do to survive." The media also usually emphasizes crime and violence because it is dramatic and exciting. If people fight over food, or steal it, we see it. During hurricanes and other disasters, many people of all colors and incomes are generous, brave, and help each other to survive — far more than the few who act badly and show up on our televisions. Most people who survived Hurricane Katrina and the Asian tsunami were heroes and helpers to each other.

7.
Answering Children's Questions about Race and Prejudice

I asked my mom how come we didn't know any poor or black people. She said they live in other places. I said we had room so one of those sad kids on TV could live with us.

JACKSON, AGE 6

Why were so many of the poor people suffering from Hurricane Katrina on television black?

Many children and adults around the world were shocked that the faces on the television screen from the flooding from Hurricane Katrina were almost entirely black. Not only are poor people largely invisible, but most Americans are living in neighborhoods effectively segregated by both social class and race. They do not often see people different from themselves.

African Americans make up a large share of the population in Louisiana (and more than 70% of the populations of New Orleans), Mississippi, and other Southern states. Many African Americans in those states are poor. Many of the people who couldn't get out of New Orleans and suffered the most were African American. Only one in four owned a car. Their faces were on television more than the hundreds of thousand of others (white and black) who were able to get out.

Why are lots of other poor people and disaster victims I see on television dark-skinned?

Many children are used to pictures of people of color suffering. The Asian tsunami happened to strike many coastal areas where many of the people had dark skin. There are also many pictures in the media of very poor people in Africa who are suffering from weather (drought, flooding), violence, or disease.

Poverty is color blind but it's not always shown that way on TV. White farmers struggling to keep their farms afloat, or poverty level white wage-earners are generally not portrayed in the media but do exist in reality.

There are also lots of dark-skinned people who are not poor, and not just celebrities like Oprah, or professional athletes, or music stars. Teachers, lawyers, doctors, business people, and all kinds of workers come in all colors too.

What is prejudice? Why do people say and do bad things about other people that they don't even know?

Prejudice is having negative feelings or ideas about a whole group of people without really knowing or understanding very much about them. It is usually based on ignorance (not knowing), fear (they could hurt me or take things I have), hate (I don't like things about them), and sometimes our own insecurity (it makes me feel better to think I am better than them).

Are there times when someone teased you about your clothes, or your hair, or for just being a girl or a boy, or for having a different skin color? Or maybe you were teased because you had different abilities and you couldn't do something. Or other children wouldn't let you play with them? Imagine feeling like that a lot of the time just because of the color of your skin?

There are people everywhere who are treated differently because they look or sound different, or have different abilities. But no one should be made to feel badly just because they look different.

What is racism and why does it happen?

Racism is treating another group of people badly because they look and act differently from you. Sometimes it is the whole community or city, state, or country that treats a group badly. In the United States, because of a long history of slavery, segregation, and racism toward African Americans, we associate most racism with the attitudes and practices of white society toward people of African heritage who have brown or black skin. There has also been racism towards people from Central and South America with brown skin, Native Americans, Asians, and people with dark skin from the Mediterranean region and Middle East. Racism also happens towards other groups around the world.

People also suffer from prejudice for reasons other than race. Sometimes religion or ethnicity is used to discriminate against people. Jewish people have had a long history of experiencing discrimination in many countries. In the United States, Irish-Americans and Italian-Americans were treated badly 100 years ago, at least in part because they were Catholic. There are prejudiced and bigoted people in every social group who act badly toward people different than themselves.

There are many groups of people that are working to end prejudice and racism. They listen to people about their feelings, try to help others see that treating others badly is wrong, and make laws to stop people from treating others badly. Do you have any ideas how we can end racism?

Why are some of the people on television so angry?

In a terrible disaster, you go through a lot. You may not have enough to eat or drink. You are tired. You might be scared and uncertain of what is going to happen next. You might have to wait and wait and wait for any kind of help, or wait a long time to simply know what is going on. You wonder if help is even coming. Sometimes you get so frustrated that you get angry, even at those who are trying to help you. Sometimes you feel that the people in charge of helping you don't know what they are doing, or just aren't trying hard enough. Television shows angry people because it is more dramatic than people who are coping without anger or are more resigned. Have you ever been so frustrated that you got angry?

Why are some of the people on television so sad?

In hurricanes, tsunamis, floods, and all disasters, people are scared and may have suffered terrible losses. They may have lost someone they love, their pet, their house, or even their whole neighborhood. They may not know what they will do now or how they will live tomorrow.

What will happen to them?

We hope that most people will get help so that their future will look brighter. Many will find out that their fears did not come true — that the people, places, or pets they cared about were not harmed, and they were reunited with most of what they had thought they lost. Others who did lose a lot will find, over time, that their sadness and hurt will go away. They will miss what they lost but will remember the good times with the people, places or pets that will live on in their memories. They will find hope for a better life.

When I grow up I am going to be a helicopter pilot or an Army man and I am going to build a house on a hill that is so strong and so big that my Momma and brothers and sisters will be safe and happy. We will have all the food and water we want.

ARTHUR, AGE 8

How can people go on when they lose so much?

People are amazing! Each of us has inside of us a strong spirit to keep going on with our life, even when terrible things happen. Sometimes that spirit is hard to find when we are sad or hurting or have almost nothing. People need other people to help them find the spirit. Family, friends, and other people like you and me can try to help those who are in need and hurting.

Have you ever felt so terrible that you wanted to just stop? What would you do if you lost your home?

8.
How Can We Feel Safe and Be Safe?

Children who have experienced a disaster directly or indirectly need reassurance that they will be safe. They have learned that nature is terrifyingly powerful. Now they need to know that no hurricane, flood, tornado, or earthquake has to harm them if they respect nature and are prepared. They need to feel in control and powerful through their own efforts and through those of the competent adults around them. The key to both feeling safe and being safe is to be prepared. The more that even very young children are involved in the process of planning safety efforts, the more they will see natural disasters as a part of life they can manage. Evacuations and fire or tornado drills can almost become family events, even if they are a little frightening.

Have a Family Meeting:

Families need to prepare and make plans for what might happen. Talk about what situations the family needs to be concerned about. Also talk about the rescuers and heroes who are there to help the family if disaster strikes.

Make a Family Plan:

Together create a family plan that covers what the family needs to do to be safe:

- Decide what will be done ahead of time to be better prepared, and who to contact (family, friends, work and school contacts).

- Develop an emergency contact list of family, friends, schools, doctors, veterinarians, police, fire, and insurance representatives.

- Create a Safety Map that includes:

    - Where to go in the house in the case of disasters where staying in is advisable
    - Evacuation plans that include where to go in or outside the neighborhood
    - How and where to check in if the family becomes separated

- Develop a Pet Survival Plan that includes scenarios for taking the pet or leaving the pet behind

- Identify guardians to take care of children if the parents are no longer able

- Take a First Aid class

Make a Family Safety Kit:

Together decide what should go in the kit and where to keep it. The kit may include:

- Flashlights and batteries
- Lighters and matches
- Candles
- First Aid kit
- Water (at least three gallons per person)
- Water purification kit or tablets
- Food (some non-perishable)
- Sleeping bags or blankets
- Radios and batteries or a radio with hand crank power
- Tarp
- Camping supplies (tent, lantern, stove, sleeping bags)
- Cash
- Medications and any necessary medical equipment
- Extra clothing
- Empty gasoline cans
- Plastic trash bags
- Copies of important documents
- Photographs of family members and family dogs or cats
- Names and numbers of important people: family, friends, doctors, and veterinarians
- Pet survival kit with pet food and water, medications, carriers and restraints, pet toys, plastic bags

Make Each Child "My Own Safety Kit:"

Have children prepare their own bags. With your help, let them decide what goes into the bag (and allow some child logic to prevail). Possible choices:

- Flashlights and batteries
- Snacks and water
- Favorites:
    - > stuffed animals and toys,
    - > pillow or blanket
    - > clothes
    - > books
    - > photographs
    - > games
    - > snacks
- Battery-powered radio and batteries
- Whistle
- Camera
- Journal
- Writing and art supplies

Have Practice Drills:

Practice what to do in the event of the possible natural disaster or fire. Assign roles for each of the children, preschool age and up. While this might sound scary to you, it will provide comfort and security to children by empowering them with skills and knowledge.

Make a Helping Plan:

Children (and adults) will feel stronger if they not only feel that they will be safe, but can also help others be safe during or after the crisis. Perhaps pack extra food, water, and supplies for others.

9. Promoting Tolerance and Respect for Others

Children can learn prejudice at a very young age. They can learn to fear differences, stereotype people, and reject others because of gender, color, race, size, culture or any of the characteristics that become the object of stereotypes, including poverty. ("Girls can't do that," Those people are dirty," "They talk funny and are stupid"). They learn this from the adults and children around them and from television, movies, music, and video games. They develop negative attitudes about groups of people and apply them to individuals. Prejudice leads to scapegoating and discrimination.

Intolerance of others begins with lack of understanding, ignorance, and fear. Education is crucial in our attempts to create a more tolerant world. Children need to be taught about humanity, human rights, poverty, and tolerance in order to combat images and stereotypes from the media and the world around them.

Children will mirror what adults say and do, which gives us the opportunity to promote tolerance. If children express fear or antagonism toward African Americans, ask them to explain what they are thinking and feeling. If they share something that doesn't sound like it came from them, ask gently where they heard it so you can offer alternative correct information. At the child's developmental level, talk about how all people, regardless of their skin color or religion or where they live, are people just like we are. For older children, explore information together about how the United States and the world is made up of many peoples of all colors.

Tolerance and respect for other cultures begins at home, but school and education are crucial to create a more understanding and tolerant world. Together, educators and families can prevent dehumanization, prejudice, and stereotyping.

- Become aware of your own biases and watch what you say about others. Be a model for respect for diversity.
- Create a multicultural environment in your home or school, and show that you value diversity in culture and social class. Expose children to other cultures and social groups through books, media, restaurants, festivals, and personal experiences with friends, coworkers, and the community.
- Use accurate and fair contemporary images of cultural groups rather than stereotypes. For example, show African Americans and Latinos who are neither poor nor famous athletes, musicians, or celebrities.
- Listen to and answer children's questions about others with respect and accuracy.
- Banish teasing or rejection, particularly when it is based on identity: gender, race, ethnicity, religion, size, age, or physical characteristics.
- Provide experiences and discussions that explore similarities between people and center on positive dimensions of difference and appreciation of them among people and cultures.

- Help children learn the difference between feeling proud of one's heritage and feeling superior to others.

- Teach children (and adults) to recognize stereotypes and caricatures so they don't use them unknowingly.

- Teach children how to challenge bias about themselves and others in non-confrontational ways.

- Help children develop their understanding of fairness and justice, as well as identify injustice.

- Encourage children to take action to make their community a better and fairer place.

Ultimately, respect and tolerance requires real relationships with real people. We must make an effort to bring children and families from different cultures together to truly come to know each other.

Adapted from *Teaching Young Children to Resist Bias: What Parents Can Do* (Sparks, et.al, NAEYC: Washington, D.C.)

10. Helping Children Grow and Thrive

Teachers and other adults who work with children are faced with many difficult issues. Life in a group setting inevitably involves accepting or reconciling different viewpoints. We all bring not only our own personalities and emotions into our work with children but our own politics, religion, and world viewpoints as well. The news may be filled with stories about people and events we have strong feelings toward or know very little about.

Crises can bring out the best and worst in each of us. The worst: selfishness and simplistic answers, blaming, avoidance, bias, or proceeding as if nothing has changed. The best: thoughtfulness, caring, kindness, courage, and the opportunity to guide children to important learning. Children learn from how people and communities respond in times of crisis. Adults need to model and teach the following:

Thoughtfulness: We need to make an effort to understand what others think and develop a broader perspective that respects the natural world and its relationship to people around the planet.

Caring: We are not alone. We live in a world of communities of children and families. Our interdependent future depends on mutual caring.

Kindness: Human beings here and around the world are hurting, and we can all take action to help in some way.

Courage: It takes courage to confront the power of nature, and to accept differences. It takes courage to help others in their confusion, fear, loss, or grief while we tend to our own.

Learning: It will help others and ourselves if we keep learning more about the world of nature, the wider world of people and culture, and the close-up world we inhabit.

Responsibility: It is our planet, our society, and our community. We need to take care of the world that we live in today and will inherit.

Finding the Strength and Goodness in Children

Disasters and crises are not only about needs. Although catastrophes may expose our frailties and vulnerabilities, they also can uncover our strengths, courage, and goodness. That is true for children as well. Author Robert Coles in *Children of Crisis: a Study of Courage and Fear* (Atlantic —Little, Brown, 1964, p.329) observed forty years ago that a middle-class parent was more interested in what was good for his children than what good he might ask of them. Coles was struck by the contrast with the "goodness" and moral courage that he saw in action as 6 year-old Ruby Bridges almost single-handedly integrated the schools of New Orleans, and other young black children all over the South joined the front lines of the American civil rights movement, facing angry mobs, water hoses, and police dogs. His observation applies today: many of us as parents spend more time trying to provide the goods and the *good life* for our children than finding the *goodness in our children.*

Even young children are capable of courage, compassion, and contributions to the community if we involve them in the life outside the home. Even the youngest can be part of a disaster relief effort. Recognizing and honoring their individual and developmental capacity and competence not only helps children cope, but is the essence of raising children to be contributing members of the society that they will inherit.

What Those Who Work With Children Can Do

While parents should use children's questions and statements as "learnable moments" to impart their moral and religious thinking and values about basic issues, teachers should help children with anxiety, confusion, or interest without expressing their own religious or political views.

Provide learning opportunities:

- Expand children's knowledge of the natural world through projects and experiments that involve growing things, measuring and tracking rain, snow, the speed of wind, or temperature.
- Provide pictures, music, films, food, art, excursions, and visitors to learn more about nature.
- Provide books at the appropriate level that address the issues of natural disasters, poverty, respect for others, conflict, and overcoming fear and adversity.
- Ensure that the curriculum includes children's current interests and concerns.

Help children cope and succeed:

- Provide materials that encourage children's play and expression of their feelings and thoughts. Children need to work through issues, so allow fantasy play or art as long as it does not hurt others.
- Value and respect individual children, and try to eliminate stressful situations when necessary (new transitions, unnecessary challenges).

Encourage an active, democratic process:

- Sustain or create a democratic group in the classroom with participatory decision-making. Make the group safe for discussion of conflicting ideas.

- Create opportunities for cooperation: projects, chores, decision-making.

Grow good people:

- Honor differences and go beyond acceptance and tolerance. Research and respect differences in identity, culture, economic differences, and beliefs.

- Notice poverty, unfairness, and injustice in daily life and the news, and call children's attention to them as appropriate.

- Encourage empathy by encouraging the safe and respectful discussion of feelings of hurt, fear, loss, and doubt (without forcing participation).

- Become sensitive to hurtful language and teach children to be alert to it.

- Try to find hope, goodness, and courage in every tragedy. Help children to see caring, courage, tolerance, and compassion in them.

Grow good citizens:

- Help children take action, and take action with them: for example, write letters, send pictures, raise money, and connect with others.

- Involve children in local and global humanitarian efforts.

Work with families:

- Treat families as partners. Keep parents and family members informed and involve them in your efforts.

11.
What Happens Now? Toward a Better World

In times of crisis it is important to find strength and reassurance in our communities, our diversity, and our common commitment to learning how to develop a better world. Horrific natural disasters that create large scale destruction can bring into focus that we are one planet — a planet that our children will inherit. How we live our lives, the resources we consume, and the policies our governments pursue, all have an effect on the natural world. Children need to be taught about nature and the earth; the natural forces that can affect our own lives and the lives of children and adults around the globe. Children need to develop an empathy and thoughtfulness that underlie their judgment. They need to learn how to work together to solve problems and draw upon the strength of their family, community, nation, and the world.

A catastrophe or crisis that spurs us to respond with compassion and support can also remind us that pain and suffering, grief or loss, are not confined to world-shattering events. Every day, children around the world need our compassion and support for tragedies and struggles both large and small.

Children are always surrounded by heroes. In addition to the firefighters, police, rescue workers, armed forces, and all those who helped the victims or survived the devastation, there are others:

- Parents, teachers, and other adults who give children their strength when they themselves are overwhelmed with their own feelings of uncertainty, fear, or grief.

- Children who help to protect themselves and their families, acting bravely as they flee or endure natural disasters.

- Children and adults who recognize they can support others in crisis and provide time, energy, or material resources to help others.

When the winds are howling, when the noise is deafening and the darkness grows, or the ground shakes or opens up, children need all the shelter and light that we can bestow upon them. We need to always remember that children have the strength and goodness within them to make the world a better place in the future.

Resources

For an updated annotated list of resources and more information on helping children cope with tragedy, visit www.brighthorizons.com.

ON DISASTERS AND RELIEF

www.aboutourkids.org
NYU Child Study Center website with articles about supporting children in the aftermath of Hurricane Katrina.

www.apa.org/pi/pii/care.html
The American Psychological Association offers resources and tips for coping after Hurricane Katrina, in English and Spanish.

www.brighthorizons.com
Bright Horizons Family Solutions has partnered with MercyCorps and JPMorgan Chase to form the Comfort for Kids project, which provides resources to children victimized by Hurricane Katrina and information about helping children cope with natural disasters and catastrophe.

www.childtrauma.org
Information and resources to help improve the lives of traumatized and maltreated children.

www.connectforkids.org
Connect for Kids provides online resources for helping people affected by Hurricane Katrina. "Emergency Guidelines for Helping Victims; Giving and Getting Help" — practical information on food drives, medical services, clothing, school supplies, and foundations collecting donations. "Help with Healing" — valuable resources for helping kids cope with trauma, explaining tragedies to children, and supporting their physical and emotional needs.

www.ed.gov/news/hurricane/index.html
The U.S. Department of Education "Hurricane Help for Schools" Web site serve as a nationwide clearinghouse to address the needs of affected schools.

www.familyinfoserv.com/pdf/anniestories.pdf
A guided self study for parents and educators to help children cope with the feelings caused by floods and other disasters.

www.mercycorps.org
An international relief and development organization whose Web site provides information on programs all over the world and shows how to get help, give help, share grief, and help children cope.

www.nasponline.org/NEAT/Katrinaparents
Advice for parents from the National Association of School Psychologists.

www.nea.org/crisis/index.html
The National Education Association's Crisis Communication Guide and Toolkit offers basic resource lists for educators.

www.networkforgood.org
The Network for Good Web site lists and explains the missions of organizations that are supporting victims of Hurricane Katrina.

www.nimh.nih.gov/publicat/violence.cfm
The National Institute of Mental Health, offering online resources to help children cope with violence and disasters.

www.nmha.org/reassurance/hurricane/children.cfm
The National Mental Health Association addresses all aspects of mental health and illness with extensive information and resources to support victims of Hurricane Katrina.

www.redcross.org
The American Red Cross provides emergency relief and immediate response to disasters. The Web site includes a wealth of suggested materials for children and teachers regarding disasters, and avenues for volunteerism or assistance.

www.smhp.psych.ucla.edu
The University of California Mental Health Project, offers broad information regarding catastrophe, tragedy, trauma, and emergencies with extensive information on the aftermath of Hurricane Katrina. Updated daily.

www.trynova.org
The National Organization for Victim Assistance provides resources and service information for victims of crimes and crises.

Children's Web Sites

www.jmu.edu/psychologydept/4kids.htm
Interactive disaster information that educates young children about floods and coping with their feelings if they are the victims of a flood disaster. Ages 4-8

www.mindohfoundation.org/hurricanekatrina.htm
MindOH! Foundation offers thought provoking, Hurricane Katrina-related lesson plans. Ages 6-12

www.ngdc.noaa.gov/seg/hazard/kqStart.shtml
The National Oceanic and Atmospheric Administration site where children can learn about and test their knowledge of natural disasters. Ages 8 and up

www.timeforkids.com/TFK/katrina
A current events online magazine that offers Katrina coverage. Ages 6-12

Books for Adults

Emotional Recovery After Natural Disasters: How to Get Back to Normal Life (An Idyll Arbor Personal Health Book), Ilana Singer. Practical information for victims of natural disasters and the people who work with them.

Children's Books

I Know What to Do: A Kid's Guide to Natural Disasters, Bonnie S. Mark, Aviva Layton and Michael Chesworth. Facts about disasters and information on how to prepare for and survive a disaster.
Age 6 and up

River Friendly, River Wild, Jane Kurtz. Narrative poems about experiences during and after the Grand Forks, North Dakota floods. Helps children understand the impact of floods and the need for collaboration. Ages 7-10

The Big Flood, Wendy Pfeffer and Vanessa Lubach. How one community responded when the Mississippi River flooded in 1993. Ages 5-9

The Flood That Came to Grandma's House, L. Stallone. Illustrates one family's ordeal when a home becomes flooded with water. Ages 4-8

The Magic School Bus: Inside a Hurricane (Magic School Bus Series), Joanna Cole and Bruce Degen. Children look inside the eye of a hurricane. Ages 4-8

Tidal Wave, Christopher Lampton. Tsunamis, their causes, and what to do if one is coming. Ages 7-10

Volcanoes: Journey to the Crater's Edge, Philippe Bourseiller. Exciting photos and drawings capture the phenomena of volcanoes in simple terms. Grades 3-6

We Shake in a Quake, Hannah Gelman Givon. Set in rhyme, the story suggests what it might be like to experience an earthquake. Includes a family earthquake preparedness list of supplies. Preschool-age 6

Quake: A Novel, Joe Cottonwood. Fourteen-year-old Franny, her younger brother, and their cousin brave the aftermath of the 1989 Loma Prieta earthquake alone. Grades 4-8

ON WEATHER

www.education-world.com
A great site for teachers with ideas and classroom activities in response to current events such as natural disasters.

www.miamisci.org/hurricane/hurricane0.html
The Miami Museum of Science gives information about hurricanes and shares survivor's stories written by children. The site includes a teacher's guide.

www.nationalgeographic.com/ngkids/
An interactive Web site where children can explore the world of nature, animals, history, space, and science. Ages 6-13

www.ncdc.noaa.gov/oa/climate/research/2005/katrina/html
The National Climatic Data Center's Climate Services gives a synopsis of the conditions that caused Hurricane Katrina.

www.realclimate.org
RealClimate is a Web site that focuses on climate science.

http://yosemite.epa.gov/OAR/globalwarming.nsf/content/ImpactsCoastalZones.html
U.S. Environmental Protection Agency article on how global warming causes the rising sea level along the coasts of the United States, and the impact on low-lying land.

Children's Web Sites

www.nws.noaa.gov/om/reachout/kidspage.shtml.org
National Weather Service Playtime for Kids offers fun interactive games and basic information designed to help kids learn about hazardous weather. All ages

www.nssl.noaa.gov/edu/bm/bm_main.html
Provides Coloring Books for Kids about Weather which helps kids learn about how to keep themselves safe. Preschool - Age 6

http://scijinks.jpl.nasa.gov/weather
An interactive Web site that helps students learns about weather while having fun. Ages 8 and up

http://volcano.und.nodak.edu/vw.html
Information and interactive activities on volcanoes. Ages 10 and up

Books for Adults

Global Warming: The Complete Briefing, John Houghton. A fairly easy read about a complicated subject matter.

The Two-Mile Time Machine: Ice Cores, Abrupt Climate Change and Our Future, Richard B. Alley. A fascinating read, telling the story of the Earth's climate history over the past 110,000 years.

Children's Books

Down Comes the Rain, Franklyn M. Branley. A concise, easy to read look at the water cycle, how water is recycled, clouds are formed, and why we have rain and hail. Grades 2-4

Flash, Crash, Rumble, and Roll, Franklyn Branley. Facts about weather and the causes of storms and a few simple experiments about weather. Grades K-4

Global Warming: Assessing the Greenhouse Threat, Laurence Pringle. In simple language, the author explains and examines the Greenhouse effect. Ages 9 -12

How the Weather Works, Michael Allaby. A sophisticated children's encyclopedia of the weather. User-friendly activities and experiments. Ages 7-12

Hurricanes, D.M. Souza. A sophisticated book describing the basics of hurricanes. Grades 3-6

Hurricanes, Sally Lee. An advanced book with scientific descriptions, understandable graphics and diagrams, and easy home activities to describe basic home preparedness in storm conditions. Grades 4-8

Hurricane and Tornado (Eyewitness Series), John Challoner. A dramatic guide that explains the destructive forces of hurricanes and tornados. Ages 8-12

Hurricanes and Tornados, Picture Library, Norman Barrett and Franklin Watts. Photographs and simple text show and explain the devastating damage that severe storms can cause. Ages 6-10

Hurricanes: Earth's Mightiest Storms, Patricia Lauber. A global lesson in hurricanes. Grades 4-8

I Face the Wind, Vicki Cobb and Julie Gorton (Illustrator). A simple, graphic book that encourages kids to observe, experiment, and learn about wind and air. Grades 2-6

It's Raining Cats and Dogs: All Kinds of Weather and Why We Have It, Franklyn Branley. Facts, folklore, and experiments about weather. Grades 3-7

Lightning, Seymour Simon. Simple text and vivid photographs explain the phenomena of lighting. Ages 5-8

No Way Out, Ivy Ruckman. A terrifying flash flood in Zion Narrows causes 7 campers to use all their resources to stay alive. Grade 7 and up

Questions and Answers About the Weather, M.J. Craig. The 50 most commonly asked questions about the weather. Ages 4-8

Shock Waves Through Los Angeles: The Northridge Earthquake, Carole G. Vogel. An excellent book that combines factual reportage, photographs, and scientific data to explain the 1994 Northridge earthquake. Grades 5-8

Storms, Seymour Simon. Clear explanation of the mechanisms that cause the destructive powers of storms. Grades 3-6

The Boy Who Held Back the Sea, Thomas Locker. A beautifully illustrated account of a young boy who saves his own town from flooding. Ages 4-8

The Day It Rained Forever, Virginia Gross. The story of the famous Johnston flood, told through the eyes of a young girl. Grades 3-5

The Storm of the Century, William Drye. A vivid account of the devastating 1935 hurricane that hit the Florida Keys. Includes victims' and survivors' stories. Grade 7- adult

Tornadoes, Ann Armbruster and Elizabeth Taylor. An overview of the scientific anatomy of tornadoes, including home experiments and activities. Grades 4-7

Tornadoes!, Arlene Erlbach. A simple 50-page illustrated reader covering the why and how of tornadoes, safety concerns, and precautions in tornado conditions. Ages 4-8

Tornadoes, Seymour Simon. Vivid photographs and words explain how tornadoes are formed, why they occur, and their destructive power. Grades 3-6

Twisters and Other Terrible Storms, Osborn W. and Osborne M. An edition of the Magic Treehouse Research Series, explains the phenomena of weather: what causes it and why, and facts about deadly storms. Ages 4-8

Weather: DK Eyewitness Guides, Brian Cosgrove. An informative guide to learn about weather. Ages 4-10

Wildfires, Seymour Simon. An easy reader which explains the natural cycle of the forest, the danger of wildfires, and safety precautions. Grades 3-5

Wild Weather: Hurricanes!, Lorraine Jean Hopping and Jody Wheeler. The authors explain the causes and effects of hurricanes. Ages 5-8

ON CHILDREN AND STRESS

http://about.com
International news Web site offering information about a wide range of topics relevant to children, families, and stress.

www.nctsnet.org
The Web site for the National Child Traumatic Stress Network contains excellent, easy to locate, important resources for parents, professionals, and the general public, regarding Hurricane Katrina and its aftermath. Many articles are available in English and Spanish.

www.nmha.org/reassurance/children.cfm
"Helping Children Handle Disaster-Related Anxiety."

www.parentleaders.org
Parent Leadership Institute is an organization that offers parent education and support.

www.preparerespondrecover.com/childrensneeds
Prepare, Respond, Recover is an organization that provides safety planning, response, and recovery support to individuals and small businesses.

www.siu.edu/departments/bushea/stress.html
Provides links to a variety of Web sites on dealing with stress in adults and children.

www.trynova.org/crisis/katrina/reactions-child.html
"Reactions of Children and Adolescents to Trauma."

Books for Adults

Helping Children Cope with Stress, Avis Brenner. Lexington: Heath & Co, 1984.

Talking to Your Kids in Tough Times: How to Answer your Child's Questions about the World We Live In, Willow Bay. New York: Warner Books, 2003.

Children's Books

A Boy and A Bear: The Children's Relaxation Book, Lori Lite and M. Hartigan. A short, well illustrated book that helps teach young children to learn relaxation techniques by breathing along with the characters. Ages 3-10

Annie Stories, Doris Brett. Fantasy stories with real life emotions and scenarios, where children can identify with the characters. Ages 4-8

Don't Despair on Thursdays, Adolph Moser and David Melton. Simple text to help children deal with grief and despair. Ages 8-12

Don't Pop Your Cork on Mondays! The Children's Anti-Stress Book, Adolph Moser and Dav Pilkey. The authors help children explore the causes and effects of stress and suggest tools to help them develop coping skills. Ages 8-12

Stress Can Really Get on Your Nerves, James J. Crist. Light humor and cartoons with serious advice to help preadolescents deal with stress. Ages 9-13

The Goodnight Caterpillar: Muscle Relaxation and Meditation Bedtime Story for Children, Improve Sleep, Manage Stress and Anxiety, Lori Lite. Captivating characters take young readers on a journey of relaxation. Ages 3-6

What to Do When You're Scared and Worried, James J. Crist. How to empower children and help them to understand, confront, and master troubling emotions. Grades 5-8

www.childtrauma.org
Provides information and resources to help improve the lives of traumatized and maltreated children.

www.dougy.org
The Dougy Center, the National Center for Grieving Children and Families, provides support and training nationally and internationally to individuals and organizations seeking to assist children in grief.

www.griefnet.org
GriefNet.org is an Internet community of professionals dealing with grief, death, and major loss. The Web site contains an extensive list of grief-related topics.

www.hospice.org
Comprehensive information for patients and families facing life threatening illnesses, death, and bereavement.

Books for Adults

Parenting through Crisis: Helping Kids in Times of Loss, Grief and Change, Barbara Coloroso. Suggestions to help parents support children through difficult times.

Children's Books

About Dying: An Open Family Book For Parents and Children Together, Sara Bonnett Stein. A thought-provoking book that uses the analogy of a pet dying to help explain the concepts of life and death. Ages 4-8

After the Funeral, Jane Loretta Winsch. This book can help children and their families move towards acceptance, understanding, and hope. Ages 4-8

Badger's Parting Gifts, Susan Varley. Badger's friends are sad when their friend dies. They treasure the memories he's left by remembering all of his gifts and relating stories about Badger. Ages 5-8

Help Me Say Goodbye: Activities for Helping Kids Cope When a Special Person Dies, Janis Silverman. Sensitive exercises (using pictures) help address the questions children may have about death. Ages 4-8

I'll Always Love You, Hans Wilhelm. A gentle, moving story about a boy loving his dog. Ages 3-7

I Miss You: A First Look at Death, Pat Thomas. A book that invites children to tell how they are feeling. Ages 4-7

I Wish I Could Hold Your Hand... A Child's Guide to Grief and Loss, Dr. Pat Palmer. A comforting book that helps grieving children identify, accept and cope with their feelings. Ages 9-12

Lifetimes, Michael Mellonie. A beautiful book to help a child see that death is a part of life. Ages 4-8

Michael Rosen's Sad Book, Michael Rosen and Quentin Blake. This touching book tells the story in pictures and words of the author's grief following the death of his son. Ages 8 and up

So Much to Think About, When Someone You Care About Has Died, Fred Rogers. This is an excellent activity book to help children and adults work out their feelings together. Ages 3-7

Tear Soup, Pat Schweibert. A richly-illustrated story about a woman who cooks up a special batch of "tear soup" after suffering a terrible loss. Ages 4-8

The Accident, Carol Carrick. Christopher must deal with his feelings of depression and guilt after his dog is hit by a truck and killed. A real and honest look at grief. Ages 4-8

The Fall of Freddie the Leaf: A Story of Life for All Ages, Leo Buscaglia, Ph.D. The author touches children and adults alike, illustrating the delicate balance between life and death. Ages 4-8

The Tenth Good Thing about Barney, Judith Viorst. After the death of his cat, a small boy (with his father's help) begins to develop an understanding of the cycle of life and how to cope with loss. Ages 4-8

The Saddest Time, Norma Simon. Three short stories about the death of an uncle, a school friend, and a grandmother, explain death as the inevitable end of life. Ages 4-8

When Dinosaurs Die: A Guide to Understanding Death, Laurie Krasny Brown and Marc Brown. In simple language, explores the feelings people may have regarding the death of a loved one and ways to honor the memories. Ages 4-8

ON HOMELESSNESS

www.brighthorizons.com/foundation
The Bright Horizons Foundation creates family/play rooms in homeless shelters.

www.copaa.org/news/hurricane.html
"Education Rights of Displaced and Homeless Children," a summary of basic legal information about the rights of students with disabilities affected by Hurricane Katrina.

www.endhomelessness.org
The National Alliance to End Homelessness is a nonprofit organization whose mission is to mobilize the nonprofit, public, and private sectors of society in an alliance to end homelessness.

http://facstaff.uww.edu/homewords/parentinhomeless
Resources and information on the impact of homelessness on children and families. It includes techniques for helping parents support (and cope with) their children, and handouts that can be used in working with parents who are homeless.

www.homesforthehomeless.com
The Institute for Children and Poverty evaluates strategies and offers innovative approaches to combat the effects of homelessness.

www.horizonsforhomelesschildren.org
Horizons for Homeless Children is a Massachusetts-based organization that works to improve the lives of homeless children and their families.

www.naehcy.org/katrina.html
National Association for the Education of Homeless Children and Youth serves as the voice for the education of homeless children, connecting educators, parents, advocates, and service providers, to ensure school success.

www.nationalhomeless.org
The National Coalition for the Homeless works to end homelessness though grassroots organizing, education, advocacy, technical assistance, and partnerships.

www.nationalhomeless.org/fmn2001/01whatdo.html
A website listing the many ways that children and schools can help children combat poverty.

www.nmha.org/homeless/childrenhomelessnessfacts.cfm
An article relaying information about the plight of homeless children.

www.serve.org.nche/
The National Center for Homeless Education provides research, resources, and information enabling communities to address the educational needs of children and youth experiencing homelessness.

Children's Books

A Shelter in our Car, Maria Teste, Karen Ritz (Illustrator). Eight-year-old Zettie and her mother left Jamaica in search of education and a better life in America, and now live in an old car. The story shows how family love thrives, regardless of where you live. Pre-k - Grade 2

Changing Places: A Kid's View of Shelter Living, Margie Chalofsky, Glen Finland, Judy Wallace, Ingrid Klass (Illustrator). A poignant view of shelter life for children. Ages 6-13

Cooper's Tale, Ralph Da Costa Nunez, Madeline Simon (Illustrator). Cooper the mouse becomes homeless and develops a friendship with three homeless children that change all their lives. Preschool

Home Is Where We Live: Life at a Shelter Through a Young Girl's Eyes, Jane Hertensten, Editor, B.L. Groth, Photographer. Life in a shelter through the eyes of a ten-year-old girl that demystifies the experience and casts as positive a light as possible on the experience. Grades 3-5

Lives Turned Upside Down, J. Hubbard. Homeless children document their lives through photographs. Grades 2 and up

No Place to Be: Voices of Homeless Children, Judith Berek. Interviews with 30 homeless children ages 8 though 18. Grade 5 and up

Our Wish, Ralph Da Costa Nunez, Jenna Mandel, Madeline Gerstein (Illustrator). After their home is destroyed, Mrs. Bun E. Rabbit and her children find themselves in need of a helping hand. Grades K-2

Sailey's Journey, Ralph Da Costa Nunez, Katrina Kwok (Illustrator). After losing his shell in a storm, Sailey the Snail joins his friends to set off on a journey to find a new home. Preschool

Someplace to Go, Ann Mc Govern, Marty Backer (Illustrator). Davey is living in a shelter and eating in a soup kitchen. The book captures his loneliness and despair, as well as hope and the happiness he feels at the end of the day when he comes home to his Mother and brother — even if it is at a shelter. Grades K-5

The Homeless Hibernating Bear, Kids Livin' Life. This story about Frankie, the hibernating bear, was written as a collaborative effort of a group of homeless children. Frankie, who gets lost in Salt Lake City, is befriended by homeless children who rescue him and return him to his mother safe and sound. Preschool

ON TOLERANCE AND BIAS

www.adl.org/education/miller/values.asp
Early Childhood Resources, Miller Early Childhood Initiative of A World of Difference Institute, Bias Free Foundations Training, on how to stop hate before it starts and learn to teach the value of "difference."

www.adl.org/bibliography
A World of Difference Web site that offers a comprehensive annotated bibliography of multi-cultural and anti-bias books for children.

www.pta.org
"What to Tell Your Child About Prejudice and Discrimination," from the National PTA, a nonprofit association of parents, educators, students, and other citizens active in their schools and communities.

www.tolerance.org
Tolerance.org is a Web project of the Southern Poverty Law Center, a nonprofit civil rights organization that promotes tolerance and diversity and combats hate and discrimination through education, inquiry, and litigation. Site features sections for teachers, parents, teens and elementary age children.

Web Sites for Children

www.peacecorps.gov/kids
Children's site sponsored by the Peace Corps. A good resource for information about cultures around the world and how to make a difference. Ages 7-13

Books and Pamphlets

Available from the Anti-Defamation League:
Anti-Defamation League
823 United Nations Plaza
New York, NY 100017

"Early Childhood Resources," Miller Early Childhood Initiative of A World of Difference Institute Bias Free Foundations

"Early Childhood Activities for Families," Miller Early Childhood Initiative of A World of Difference Institute Bias Free Foundations

Close the Book on Hate: 101 Ways to Combat Prejudice. ADL and Barnes & Nobel, NY, 2000.

"What to Tell Your Child About Prejudice and Discrimination" (pamphlet)

Hate Hurts: How Children Learn and Unlearn Prejudice, ADL, Caryl Stern-LaRosa, and Ellen Hofheimer Bettmann. NY, Scholastic, 2000.

Books for Adults

Caring and Capable Kids, Linda Williams. An activity book filled with stories, songs and worksheets to help children develop empathy and compassion, and learn to exercise sound judgment. Grades K-8

The Affective Curriculum, Teaching the Anti-bias Approach to Young Children, Nadia Saderman and Valerie Rhomberg. Both a theoretical and practical approach that helps teachers develop skills to foster anti-bias attitudes in children. It includes activities for infants, toddlers, preschool and school age children, international resources and a dictionary of useful terms translated into 20 languages.

Teaching Your Child to Resist Bias; brochure from NAEYC. (available at 800-424-2460 or www.naeyc.org).

Anti Bias Curriculum: Tools for Empowering Young Children, Louise Derman Sparks.

Roots and Wings: Affirming Culture in Early Childhood Programs, Stacey York.

Working with Children from Culturally Diverse Backgrounds, Diane Klien and Deborah Chen.

Children's Books

Black, White, Just Right, Marguerite W. Davol, Irene Trivas (Illustrator). A playful picture book in which a mixed race child talks about the rich differences in her family — but they're all "just right." Preschool

Erik is Homeless, Keith Elliot Greenberg. A photo essay and story of hope about Erik's life in shelters and at welfare hotels. Ages 5-9

Fly Away Home, Eve Bunting. A picture book about the lives of a boy and his father who live at the airport. Ages 4-8

Let's Talk About Race, Lester Julius, Karen Barbour (Illustrator). The author introduces the concept of race as only one component of a person's or nation's story. Grades 1-5

The Best Part of Me, Wendy Ewald. Ethnically diverse fourth and fifth grade children talk about their bodies in pictures and words. Ages 4-8

The Colors of Us, Karen Katz. Seven-year-old Lena and her mother observe the variations of colors in people, viewed in terms of things found in nature and foods. Preschool - grade 2

The Skin I'm In, Sharon J. Flake. A powerful novel that encourages children to accept differences in skin color and other racial characteristics. Grades 6-8

Trevor's Story: Growing Up Biracial, Bethany Kandel. Ten-year-old Trevor talks about his life and how it feels to be the son of a white mother and a black father. Ages 4-8

Why Are All the Black Kids Sitting Together in the Cafeteria? Beverly Daniel Tatum. This book offers insight into American culture and experiences with race and racism in everyday life.
High school - adult